apple

WATERFORD TOWNSHIP
PUBLIC LIBRARY

W9-BYH-687

DISCARD

58254

Atoms, molecules, and states of
matter
YA 539.7 ATO

FACTS AT YOUR
FINGERTIPS

INTRODUCING CHEMISTRY
ATOMS, MOLECULES, AND STATES OF MATTER

BROWN
BEAR
BOOKS

CONTENTS

Published by Brown Bear Books Limited

4877 N. Circulo Bujia
Tucson, AZ 85718
USA

and

First Floor
9-17 St. Albans Place
London N1 ONX
UK

www.brownreference.com

© 2010 The Brown Reference Group Ltd

Library of Congress Cataloging-in-Publication Data

Atoms, molecules, and states of matter / edited by Graham Bateman.
    p. cm. — (Facts at your fingertips)
  Includes index.
  ISBN 978-1-936333-10-3 (lib. bdg.)
 1. Matter—Constitution—Juvenile literature. 2. Matter—Properties—Juvenile literature. I. Bateman, Graham. II. Title. III. Series.

  QC173.16.A86 2010
  539.7—dc22

                                    2010016427

All rights reserved. This book is protected by copyright.
No part of it may be reproduced, stored in a retrieval system, or transmitted in any form or by any means, without the prior permission in writing of the publisher, nor be otherwise circulated in any form of binding or cover other than that in which it is published and without a similar condition including this condition being imposed on the subsequent publisher.

ISBN-13 978-1-936333-10-3

Editorial Director: Lindsey Lowe
Project Director: Graham Bateman
Design Manager: David Poole
Designer: Steve McCurdy
Text Editors: Peter Lewis, Briony Ryles
Indexer: David Bennett
Children's Publisher: Anne O'Daly
Production Director: Alastair Gourlay

Printed in the United States of America

Picture Credits
Abbreviations: SS=Shutterstock; c=center; t=top; l=left; r=right.
Cover Images
Front: SS: James Thew
Back: istockphoto: Chris Boy

1 SS: Przemyslaw Skibinsk; 3 SS: Morten Hilmer; 4 SS: Przemyslaw Skibinski; 6 SS: Mitzy; 8-9 SS: Ventin; 9 Photos.com; 10 SS: Ventin; 12-13 Wikimedia Commons: CERN; 14 SS: Peter Gudella; 17 SS: Immelstorm; 18 SS: Morten Hilmer; 20-21 SS: TOPS Photo; 21 SS: Jose Ignacio Soto; 22 SS: Dariush M.; 25 SS: DMM Photography, Designs & Art; 27 SS: Patrick Poencdl; 28 Wikimedia Commons: United States Department of Energy; 31 SS: Bork; 32-33 Great Images of NASA; 35 SS: Bestweb; 36 SS: Mircea Bezergheanu; 38-39 SS: Andy Lim; 41 SS: Galyna Andrushko; 42 Photos.com; 44t SS: Dole; 44b SS: Anastas Dimitrov; 46 SS: Zhiltsov Alexandr; 48 SS: Gunnar Pippel; 50-51 SS: Hiroshi Ichkawa; 52-53 SS: Slovodan Miskovic; 55 Wikimedia Commons; 56 SS: Joel Shawn; 58 SS: Saponjic.

Artwork © The Brown Reference Group Ltd

The Brown Reference Group Ltd has made every effort to trace copyright holders of the pictures used in this book. Anyone having claims to ownership not identified above is invited to contact The Brown Reference Group Ltd.

Facts at your Fingertips—Introducing Chemistry describes the essentials of chemistry from the fundamentals of atomic structure, through the periodic table, to descriptions of different types of reactions and the properties of elements, including industrial applications for chemical processes.

Everything in the universe is made of matter. In *Atoms, Molecules, and States of Matter*, the detailed structure and properties of the building blocks of matter (atoms) is described, followed by how atoms bond to produce the various types of molecules. Matter exists either in liquid, solid, or gaseous forms— here the properties of these states are reviewed in detail, including how they mix and form solutions, and how they can change state by the addition or removal of energy.

Numerous explanatory diagrams and informative photographs, detailed features on related aspects of the topics covered and the main scientists involved in the advancement of chemistry, and definitions of key "Science Words," all enhance the coverage. "Try This" features outline experiments that can be undertaken as a first step to practical investigations.

WHAT IS MATTER?

Everything in the universe is made from matter. Matter is made up of tiny building blocks called atoms. Chemistry is the science that investigates how atoms are organized to make the huge variety of substances we see around us.

ELEMENT, MIXTURE, COMPOUND

Substances exist in different forms in nature. At the most basic level are substances known as elements. Elements consist of one type of atom. These atoms may be single atoms or molecules containing a number of atoms. Mixtures occur when molecules of different substances mingle together, but do not combine physically or chemically. The ingredients of a mixture can be separated from each other. Compounds are the result of a chemical reaction between two or more substances and can only be separated into individual elements by chemical methods.

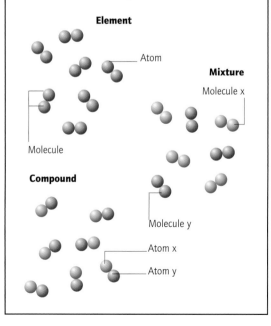

Element

Atom

Molecule

Mixture

Molecule x

Compound

Molecule y

Atom x

Atom y

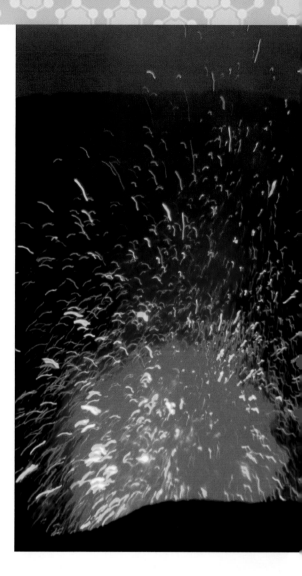

Everything around you is made of matter. The pages of this book, the air you breathe, and even your body are made from the same building blocks. These building blocks do not make up just the things on Earth. Everything in the universe—the Sun, the billions of other stars, rocks, and clouds of dust, are made of them, too.

Introducing atoms

The building blocks of matter are called atoms. Atoms are tiny and are far too small to see. About 125 million atoms lined up in a single row would be an inch long. However, not all atoms are the same. There are 92 different types in nature. Atoms come in different sizes and masses and have many properties.

Erupting volcanoes show matter in all three states—the solid rock that forms the volcano, the liquid magma that pours out of it, and the gases that are blasted into the atmosphere.

Atoms group together to make the objects and other materials around us. Matter that contains just one type of atom is called an element. For example, a gold nugget contains only gold atoms. Other elements include carbon, iron, aluminum, sulfur, and oxygen.

Molecules

Elements are unique materials because they cannot be broken up into simpler ingredients. However, not everything in the universe is made of pure elements. Most things contain combinations of the atoms of several different elements. Combinations of different types of atoms are called compounds.

When the atoms group together, they make a structure called a molecule. A molecule has a unique shape and size. This gives a material certain properties, such as making it hard or bendable. Compounds frequently have properties that are different from those of the elements included in the molecule. For example, as an element, sodium is a soft metal that reacts violently with water. Chlorine is a highly reactive gas. When combined as common table salt, sodium and chlorine form a glassy crystal that is stable, safe, and unreactive at room temperature.

SCIENCE WORDS

- **Atom:** The smallest independent building block of matter.
- **Element:** A material that cannot be broken up into simpler ingredients.
- **Gas:** State in which particles are not joined and are free to move in any direction.
- **Liquid:** State in which particles are loosely bonded and are able to move freely around each other.
- **Molecule:** Two or more joined atoms that have a unique shape and size.
- **Solid:** Matter in which particles are held in a rigid arrangement.
- **State:** The form that matter takes—either a solid, a liquid, or a gas.

States of matter

All matter has three basic forms, or states: solid, liquid, and gas. There is a fourth state of matter, called plasma, but most of the material on Earth tends to exist as a solid, a liquid, or a gas.

A material can change from one state to another by being heated or cooled. Solids melt into liquids, and liquids evaporate into gases. In the opposite direction, gases condense into liquids, which then freeze into solids.

STATES OF MATTER

Solid

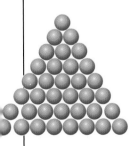

The particles are held strongly together. This example (left) is a rigid crystal structure. The particles can move, but only vibrate back and forth inside the crystal.

Liquid

The particles are less tightly packed than in a solid. They can move past each other, so a liquid can flow into different shapes.

Gas

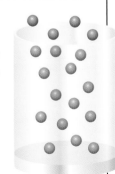

The particles are not joined to any other. All move independently of each other. A gas will spread out to fill all available space.

The elements are the basic substances in nature. They cannot be broken down into simpler substances. Each element has its own type of atom of a particular size and mass (amount of matter) and with certain characteristic chemical properties.

Not all atoms are the same. There are 92 types of atoms that occur naturally on Earth, and they make up the most basic substances called elements. Three-quarters of the elements are metals. Ten other elements are gases in normal conditions, while just two (including one of the metals) are liquids. Some elements will react with just about all the others, while a few rarely react at all.

EARTHY ELEMENTAL FACTS

The most common element in the universe is hydrogen. Hydrogen atoms are the smallest and simplest of all atoms. Three-quarters of all matter in the universe is made of hydrogen.

The most common element on Earth is iron. Much of the planet's core is made of this metal. However, the most common elements on the surface of Earth are silicon and oxygen. For example, silicon dioxide is the main compound in sand and is also found in most rocks. Other elements are very rare indeed. For example, there is just 1 ounce (28 g) of astatine in all of Earth's rocks put together.

Liquid iron and nickel outer core.

Solid mantle made of iron, magnesium, aluminum, silicon, and compounds of oxygen and silicon. Divided into upper mantle and lower mantle.

Solid iron and nickel inner core.

Continental and oceanic floor crust made of aluminum, calcium, silicon, and oxygen compounds.

Earth is made of several layers comprising different elements and compounds. Iron is the most common element on Earth and may be either solid or liquid, depending on pressure and temperature.

It is possible that more than 92 elements occur elsewhere in the universe, but these only last for a short time before breaking down into more stable elements. None of these unstable elements exist naturally on Earth any more. Scientists have made some of them in laboratories, but they can only produce very tiny amounts at a time and they quickly break down.

Discovering elements

People have long understood that certain basic substances can be combined to make new and completely different substances. Today, chemists understand how atoms are constructed and what makes each element different from the next. However,

Bismuth is a rare metallic element with a regular crystalline structure. Its pattern of interlocking squares and rainbow colors makes it one of the most distinctive elements.

before science provided these explanations, people had very different ideas about elements.

For many hundreds of years, people thought that everything in the world was made from just four elements: earth, fire, water, and air. The way these were supposed to work had more to do with magic than science. Nevertheless the idea of elements as fundamental substances was not incorrect, it was just that nobody had discovered any of the true elements.

The birth of chemistry

The first people to investigate how materials could be changed into other substances were not chemists but alchemists. Alchemists are first recorded working in Egypt and China about 2,500 years ago. Alchemists were not scientists and much of what they did is often remembered as the work of wizards and witches. They made potions and remedies and thought that matter could be transformed using magic.

WATERFORD TOWNSHIP PUBLIC LIBRARY

110858

SCIENCE WORDS

- **Alchemist:** Person who tried to change one substance into another using a combination of primitive chemistry and magic.
- **Four elements:** The ancient theory that all matter consisted of only four elements (earth, air, fire, and water) and their combinations.

Unlike chemists, alchemists did not carry out proper scientific experiments. They also did not understand many of the basic principles of chemistry, such as the difference between a compound and a mixture. Even so, they did make some important discoveries. For instance, alchemists began to understand that there were many more than just four elements. They also identified several of the metal elements, such as mercury, iron, and gold. In addition, alchemists correctly speculated that sulfur, arsenic, and other nonmetals were elements. They began to use different symbols for each of the elements, and modern chemists do the same. Yet nobody really understood that elements were made of atoms and formed compounds until chemists began to investigate elemental properties in a scientific way.

Invisible atoms

Atoms have only been detected by scientists in the last 100 years or so. However, people have been talking about atoms for thousands of years. The first people to think atoms existed were ancient Greek philosophers. Unlike alchemists, philosophers did not perform any experiments to understand matter. They did not use science to prove their ideas, either. Instead they came up with theories that seemed to match the way they observed nature working.

The word atom comes from the Greek word *atomos*, which means "indivisible." The first person to suggest that matter is made up of atoms was Leucippus of Miletus, who lived about 2,500 years ago. He thought

Mercury is a metallic element and is one of only two elements that are liquid at room temperature—the other is bromine.

atoms were all the same and could not be squeezed, stretched, or broken. Leucippus believed atoms had to exist because things were constantly changing in nature. However, he understood that something new could not be made from nothing, so he suggested that all changes were just atoms being rearranged. The atoms themselves could not be changed, only the way in which they were organized. Leucippus and his followers did not understand anything about how atoms are constructed or why they behave the way they do. However, their atom theory was correct in many ways.

GIBBERING ALCHEMISTS

Alchemists were very different from modern chemists. Chemists are scientists and they share their discoveries with others. Chemists check each other's discoveries to make sure they are correct and then use them to learn more about how atoms and molecules behave.

In contrast, the main goal of an alchemist was to find one of three things: the elixir, a drink that could make a person live forever; the panacea, a medicine that could cure all illnesses; and the philosopher's stone, which could turn any metal into gold. Obviously these discoveries would have made an alchemist hugely powerful. As a result, alchemists preferred to keep their work private. They recorded things in code, using strange symbols.

One of the most influential alchemists was the Arab Jabir ibn Hayyan (*c.* 721-*c.* 815), also known as Geber. His writings are very confusing and they often contradict each other. The word gibberish, meaning "to talk nonsense," comes from this man's name.

This engraving depicts an alchemist surrounded by the apparatus, instruments, and books of magic that he would use to carry out experiments and create potions. In the 18th century, as scientific knowledge increased, alchemy began to be replaced by chemistry.

Scientific approach

When chemists began to study substances in a scientific way, they began to realize that matter was indeed made of atoms, but that not all atoms were the same. John Dalton (1766-1844) was an English scientist who made one of the greatest discoveries in chemistry. At the beginning of the 19th century, he noticed that when two types of gases were mixed together, they did not behave as a single cloud that filled its container. Leucippus had said that all things were made up of identical atoms, so why were the atoms in each gas behaving differently? Dalton saw that both gases expanded independently of each other, so they were both spread evenly throughout the container. This simple observation proved that not all atoms were the same, as Leucippus had thought. The two gases must contain different types of atoms that behave differently from each other.

Weights and measures

By the early 19th century, scientists had identified about 25 elements. These included metals such as gold, mercury, and copper, which had been known for centuries. There were also new additions, including oxygen, which had been discovered a few years before Dalton's experiment. Dalton suggested that each element had its own type of atom.

The main difference Dalton could find between the various elements was their mass (how much matter the substance contains) and density (how much mass something has at a particular volume). He figured out how heavy an element was by reacting it with a fixed mass of another element. He then weighed what was produced and could calculate how heavy the first element was compared with the second. The extra mass of the new compound indicated how heavy the added atoms were. With this measurement, Dalton could begin to figure out how heavy each type of atom was in relation to all the others.

Dalton also showed that compounds formed from even proportions of elements. For example, a compound could contain equal amounts of two elements, or have twice as much of one than the other. However, the proportions of each ingredient were always whole numbers. You never find one atom of an element joined to one and a half atoms of another element.

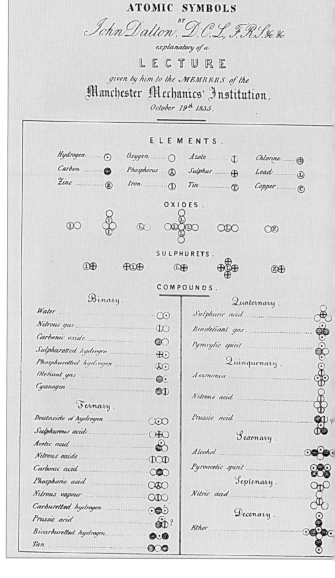

SCIENCE WORDS

- **Chemical formula:** The letters and numbers that represent a chemical compound, such as "H_2O" for water.
- **Chemical symbol:** The letters that represent a chemical, such as "Cl" for chlorine or "Na" for sodium.

Symbols and formulas

Although he did not know it at the time, Dalton was describing how atoms are arranged inside a compound's molecules. A simple compound such as sodium chloride (common salt) is produced when equal amounts of sodium and chlorine atoms react together. The proportion of each element, or ratio, is 1:1. However, other compounds have more complicated ratios of elements. For example, water is formed when hydrogen and oxygen react. Twice as many hydrogen atoms are needed as oxygen atoms. So the compound has a ratio of 2:1.

This table of elements, compounds, and chemical symbols was created by English scientist John Dalton in 1808. Each circular symbol represents one atom, and molecules are represented by combinations of these symbols. This system is no longer used, but many of Dalton's ideas were essentially correct.

Chemists use these proportions to explain the exact ingredients of molecules. Like alchemists before them, chemists use symbols for each element. However, they have chosen ones that are much easier to understand. The symbol of hydrogen is H; chlorine is Cl; and oxygen has the symbol O. Some elements have less obvious symbols because they are taken from languages other than English. For example, sodium has the symbol Na, which comes from the Latin word *natrium*. Iron has the symbol Fe from *ferrum*, the Latin word for iron. The symbol for mercury is Hg, which comes from the Greek word *hydrargyros* (meaning literally "liquid silver').

Chemists combine the symbols and the proportions to make chemical formulas. These are a way of describing what proportions of elements a compound contains. For example, the formula for sodium chloride is NaCl. Water has the formula H_2O. The subscript 2 indicates that in each molecule of water, two hydrogen atoms are joined with one oxygen atom. More complicated compounds, such as glucose (a type of sugar), have large molecules containing many atoms. The formula for glucose is $C_6H_{12}O_6$.

MOLECULES AND FORMULAS

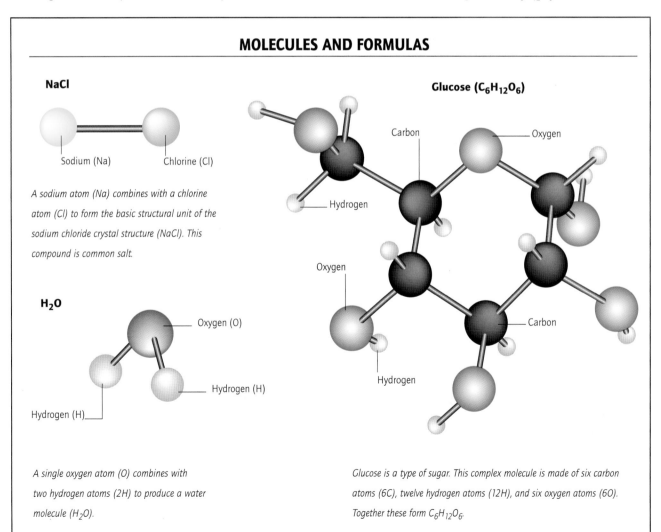

NaCl

Sodium (Na) Chlorine (Cl)

A sodium atom (Na) combines with a chlorine atom (Cl) to form the basic structural unit of the sodium chloride crystal structure (NaCl). This compound is common salt.

H_2O

Oxygen (O)

Hydrogen (H)

Hydrogen (H)

A single oxygen atom (O) combines with two hydrogen atoms (2H) to produce a water molecule (H_2O).

Glucose ($C_6H_{12}O_6$)

Carbon Oxygen

Hydrogen

Oxygen

Carbon

Hydrogen

Glucose is a type of sugar. This complex molecule is made of six carbon atoms (6C), twelve hydrogen atoms (12H), and six oxygen atoms (6O). Together these form $C_6H_{12}O_6$.

LOOKING AT ATOMS

An element's properties come from the way it is made. Each element is made up of particular atoms. Tiny atoms are themselves made up of even smaller particles. Each element has a unique number of these particles inside each of its atoms.

For hundreds of years, scientists thought that atoms were the smallest particles of matter. In the 20th century, scientists began to realize that atoms were made of even smaller particles called subatomic particles. There are three types of subatomic particles in atoms. These are protons, neutrons, and electrons. All atoms are constructed using these particles, which are always arranged following the same rules. An element's physical and chemical properties are set by the number of particles in its atoms. For example, an element with many particles in its atoms will be very dense. However, an element with just a few particles in its atoms will have a low density. Similarly, the number of particles in an element's atoms governs how reactive the element is.

SCIENCE WORDS

- **Atomic mass number:** The number of protons and neutrons in an atom's nucleus.
- **Atomic number:** The number of protons in a nucleus.
- **Electron:** A small, negatively charged subatomic particle that circles the nucleus.
- **Neutron:** A subatomic particle with no charge located in an atom's nucleus.
- **Nucleus:** The central part of an atom, made of protons and neutrons.
- **Proton:** A positively charged particle found in an atom's nucleus.
- **Subatomic particles:** Particles that are smaller than an atom.

Protons

The inside of an atom is mostly empty space, and the particles inside it are incredibly small. At the center is a tiny core called the nucleus (plural, nuclei). The nucleus contains the first type of particle: the proton. The name proton was first used to describe this particle around 1920 and comes from the Greek word for "first." The proton was given this name because it was the first particle to be found inside an atom. (Electrons were discovered in 1897, but they were not known to be part of atoms until after the discovery of protons.)

The number of protons in an atom defines the type of element. The simplest and smallest type of atoms—those of hydrogen—have just a single proton in their nucleus. Larger atoms have more protons in the nucleus. For example, the largest naturally occurring element is the metal uranium. Uranium atoms have 92 protons. The number of protons in an atom is called the atomic number. Each element has a unique number of protons in its nucleus. If two atoms have different atomic numbers, then they belong to different elements.

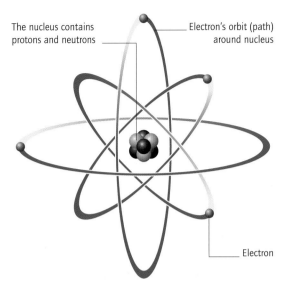

The nucleus contains protons and neutrons

Electron's orbit (path) around nucleus

Electron

An atom is mostly empty space. The protons and neutrons are gathered in the central region called the nucleus. The electrons orbit the nucleus.

These curves and spirals show the paths of subatomic particles recorded by a machine called a particle detector.

Protons have a positive electrical charge. This charge is a fundamental property of protons, and each one has an identical charge. Chemists describe the charge of each proton as +1.

A proton's charge is linked to the way it pushes and pulls on other particles inside the atom. Because of the protons contained within it, a nucleus always has a positive charge. The nucleus of a larger atom contains a lot of protons. Because of this, the charges of these particles add up to make a positive charge that is stronger than that of a smaller nucleus, which has fewer protons.

Neutrons

With the exception of hydrogen, all elements have a second type of particle in their nuclei. These are called neutrons. Neutrons are slightly heavier than protons. However, they have no electrical charge—they are neutral. Because they have no charge, neutrons do not play much of a role in chemical reactions.

The simplest element to have neutrons in its atoms is helium. This has two protons in the nucleus and two neutrons. The number of neutrons in larger atoms is also roughly the same as the number of protons. However, this varies a lot from element to element. The number of particles in an atom's nucleus—protons plus neutrons—is called the atomic mass number. For example, most hydrogen atoms have an atomic mass

TINY PARTICLES

Subatomic particles are extremely small. One gram of electrons contains more than a 1,000 times more individual particles in it than there are stars in the entire universe. (Astronomers think there are about ten thousand billion billion stars in all.)

The largest atoms are about five millionths of a millimeter across. However, the nucleus, where most of the atom's mass is located, is just a few trillionths of a millimeter across. That is like a ping-pong ball positioned in the center of a sports stadium.

number of 1 (1 proton plus 0 neutrons) and most carbon atoms have atomic mass numbers of 12 (6 protons and 6 neutrons). The atomic mass number tells scientists how much matter is contained inside an atom and how heavy it is.

Electrons

The third type of subatomic particle, the electron, is not located in the nucleus. Instead, electrons move around (orbit) the nucleus. Electrons are about 1,830 times lighter than a proton or neutron.

Despite their small size, electrons have a negative electrical charge of –1. This charge is exactly equal and opposite to the charge of each proton. Particles that have opposite charges attract each other, and the negatively charged electrons are pulled toward the positively charged nucleus. This force keeps the electrons in position and holds the atom together.

Aluminum has many common uses, such as in soft drinks cans. Each of the tiny aluminum atoms is made of a nucleus of 13 protons and 14 neutrons surrounded by 13 electrons.

The number of electrons in an atom is always the same as the number of protons. For example, hydrogen atoms have one electron, while helium atoms have two. Therefore, the positive charge of the protons is balanced exactly by the charge of the electrons. As a result, whole atoms never have an overall charge.

Varying numbers

All the atoms of one element must have the same atomic number. However, atoms of the same element can have slightly different atomic mass numbers. That is because an element can have different numbers of neutrons in its nuclei. The different versions of an element are called isotopes.

Hydrogen atoms, for example, exist as three isotopes. Most of them are simple hydrogen atoms with an atomic mass number of 1 (they have a single proton in the nucleus). About 0.015 percent of

ATOMIC STRUCTURE

The number of protons in the nucleus of an atom determines the type of element the atom is. The number of neutrons is usually similar to the number of protons, but is not always the same. Protons and electrons have an electric charge. The protons are positively charged and the electrons are negatively charged. Neutrons are electrically neutral; they have no charge.

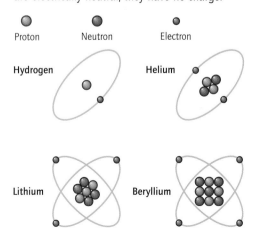

Proton   Neutron   Electron

Hydrogen   Helium

Lithium   Beryllium

SCIENCE WORDS

- **Alpha particle:** The nucleus of a helium atom. This particle has two protons and two neutrons.
- **Isotope:** Atoms of a given element always have the same number of protons, but can have different numbers of neutrons. These different versions of the same element are called isotopes.

hydrogen atoms have a neutron as well as a proton in the nucleus. This isotope has an atomic mass number of two and is named deuterium, or heavy hydrogen. Finally, one in every billion trillion hydrogen atoms is the isotope tritium. This has two neutrons in the nucleus and so has an atomic mass number of 3.

Displaying isotopes

To ensure that people know what isotope an atom is, an atom's atomic mass number is always written above its symbol, and the atomic number is displayed below it. For example the main isotope of carbon is displayed as $^{12}_{6}$C. This isotope is also described as carbon-12 (C-12).

The atoms of both deuterium and tritium are radioactive. This means that their nuclei are unstable and they quickly break apart, releasing radiation (see pages 28–31). Many of the less common isotopes of other elements are radioactive, too.

Calculating atomic mass

Chemists use a system of atomic masses based on the mass of each element that will react with a known mass of another. In effect, they are using an average mass based on the relative amount of each isotope of an element present. For example, most hydrogen atoms have an atomic mass number of 1, but a tiny amount of the element's atoms have atomic mass numbers of 2 and 3. Therefore the average atomic mass number for all hydrogen atoms is very slightly higher than 1

DISCOVERING ATOMIC STRUCTURE

Electrons were discovered in 1897, protons in 1910, and neutrons in 1932. At first scientists thought that atoms were more or less solid arrangements of protons with the smaller electrons positioned in between to balance out the particles' different charges. But in 1911, chemist Ernest Rutherford (1871–1937) showed that protons were actually confined to a tiny nucleus at the center of the atom. He discovered this by firing a beam of alpha particles at a very thin sheet of gold. (An alpha particle is the nucleus of a helium atom that has lost its electrons. It has two protons and two neutrons and is positively charged.) Most particles went straight through the gold, but some were deflected and others bounced back. Rutherford realized that the particles that were changing direction were being repelled by other positively charged particles inside the atom. The fact that the beam was only affected by very tiny areas of the gold sheet (areas smaller than the size of individual atoms) led him to conclude that protons—the positively charged parts of atoms—only occupy a tiny area at the center of the atom, which he called the nucleus.

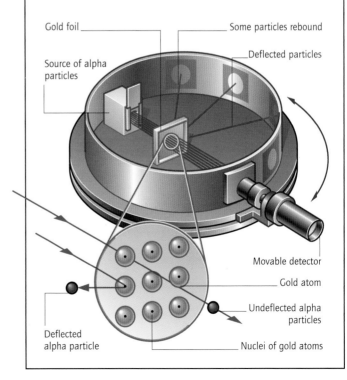

Gold foil

Source of alpha particles

Some particles rebound

Deflected particles

Movable detector

Gold atom

Undeflected alpha particles

Deflected alpha particle

Nuclei of gold atoms

ISOTOPES

Hydrogen exists as three isotopes. By far the most common isotope is ($_1^1$H). This has only a single proton in its nucleus and no neutrons. Deuterium ($_1^2$H) and tritium ($_1^3$H) are much rarer. They have one and two neutrons in their nucleus respectively. Unlike the isotopes of hydrogen, most isotopes do not have special names and are therefore identified by their atomic number, such as carbon-12 ($_6^{12}$C) and carbon-14 ($_6^{14}$C). The number of electrons does not change in different isotopes of the same element. The electron number remains the same as that of the atomic number (proton number).

Proton

Neutron

Electron

Hydrogen (mass 1)

Carbon-12 (mass 12)

Deuterium (mass 2)

Carbon-14 (mass 14)

Tritium (mass 3)

(1.00794 to be precise). This number is the element's atomic mass. To keep things simple, chemists often round down hydrogen's atomic mass to just 1.

Amedeo Avogadro

Amedeo Avogadro was born in Turin, Italy, on August 9, 1776. His father, Count Filippo Avogadro, was a lawyer, and Amedeo also trained as a lawyer, but he became increasingly interested in physics and mathematics. In 1806, he was appointed demonstrator at the Academy of Turin. In 1811, he published a paper in which he suggested that equal volumes of gases at the same temperature and pressure contain the same number of molecules. This paper was to have a great influence on chemistry, although it was many years before the importance of his work was widely recognized. Avogadro's number is named in honor of his important contribution to the understanding of atoms and molecules, though he had no knowledge of this number or of the mole.

Relative atomic mass

Atoms are extremely light—a hydrogen atom weighs about 1.7 trillion trillionths of a gram. It would be very confusing to use units this small to compare one atom with another. Instead an atom's mass is expressed as a comparison with the masses of other elements' atoms.

Chemists do this using atomic mass numbers. For example, hydrogen has an atomic mass of 1, helium has an atomic mass of 4, while carbon has an atomic mass of 12. This shows that carbon atoms are 12 times heavier than hydrogen atoms and three times heavier than helium atoms. Chemists often refer to atomic mass as relative atomic mass (RAM) because that name explains that the figure relates to the other elements.

Molecules contain more than one atom, and their mass is also important. This mass is measured as the total of the atomic masses of the atoms in the molecule. This adds up into the relative molecular mass (RMM). For example, a water molecule has two hydrogen atoms (atomic mass 1) and one oxygen atom (atomic mass 16). Therefore water's RMM is 18 (1+1+16). Knowing the RAMs and RMMs of different substances helps chemists figure out how those substances have combined and altered during chemical reactions.

Moles

Chemists measure amounts of elements and compounds using a unit called a mole. The mole is defined as 12 grams (0.42 ounces) of carbon-12 atoms. (The RAM of this isotope is 12). Chemists chose this isotope to define the mole because carbon is a common element on Earth. One mole of any element has a mass equivalent to its atomic mass expressed in grams. For example, one mole of hydrogen has a mass of 1 gram (0.035 oz), while one mole of lead, which has an atomic mass of 207, has a mass of 207 grams (7.3 oz).

A mole of anything contains the same number of particles or pieces—602,213,670,000,000,000,000,000. This number is more often written as 6.022×10^{23}, which means 6.022 multiplied by 10, 23 times. This is about 10 times the number of stars there are thought to be in the entire universe. This number is called Avogadro's number. It is named for the Italian scientist Amedeo Avogadro (1776–1856). Avogadro suggested that equal quantities of gases at a fixed temperature and pressure always contain the same number of atoms or molecules. Therefore a gallon of hydrogen gas contains the same number of atoms as a gallon

TRY THIS

How many molecules?
Water has an RMM of 18. One mole of water has a mass of 18 grams (0.6 oz). You can use this to calculate how many molecules a cup of water contains. Weigh an empty cup on a kitchen scale; using grams makes it easier. Pour some water into the cup and see how much heavier it is. The difference is the mass of the water. Divide this mass in grams by 18 to get the number of moles of water in the cup. Then multiply this figure by Avogadro's number to calculate the number of molecules. For example, if the water has a mass of 36 grams, then there are 2 moles that together contain 1.204 trillion trillion molecules.

of oxygen gas. However, the gallon of oxygen has a mass 16 times more than the gallon of hydrogen.

Using Avogadro's number, relative atomic mass numbers, and relative molecular mass numbers, chemists can easily figure out the number of atoms or molecules in a given sample.

Crystals of copper sulfate ($CuSO_4$). The relative molecular mass (RMM) for this compound can be calculated by adding the relative atomic masses (RAM) of each element. Copper (Cu) has a RAM of 64, sulfur (S) 32, and oxygen (O) 16. So, taking into account that $CuSO_4$ has four oxygen atoms, the RMM is 64 + 32 + (4 x 16) = 160.

SCIENCE WORDS

- **Mole:** The number of atoms in 12 grams of carbon-12 atoms. This number is 6.022×10^{23}.
- **Relative atomic mass (RAM):** A measure of the mass of an atom compared with the mass of another atom. The values used are the same as those for atomic mass.
- **Relative molecular mass (RMM):** The sum of all the atomic masses of the atoms in a molecule.

UNDERSTANDING ELECTRONS

Electrons play an important role in chemical reactions. Their arrangement around an atom influences how easily an element will combine with other elements. They are also responsible for the production of light.

While most of an atom's matter is locked up in the dense nucleus at the center, most of its behavior is controlled by the tiny electrons that move around the nucleus. For example, electrons are the parts of the atom that are involved in chemical reactions.

Arranging electrons

Each electron in an atom has its own position. The electrons repel each other and never come into contact. They are also arranged in layers, called electron shells. Different atoms have a different number of shells, depending on how many electrons the atom has.

For example, hydrogen has just a single shell, containing its only electron. However, the atoms of uranium, the largest element, have their 92 electrons arranged in seven shells. The shell nearest the nucleus is the smallest. Shells get larger and can hold more electrons as they get farther away from the center of the atom.

Energy levels

Electron shells are also sometimes described as energy levels. The electrons in the shell nearest to the nucleus have the lowest amount of energy, and those farthest away have the highest. When an atom receives some energy, such as when it is heated, its electrons move to a higher energy level farther away from the nucleus. Atoms release energy when their electrons drop down to lower energy levels and move back toward the nucleus. This model of how an atom works was suggested by Niels Bohr (1885–1962), a Danish physicist, in 1913. It is still seen as one of the best ways to understand atoms.

The Sun releases particles that travel through space as the solar wind. When such a stream hits Earth, the particles in the solar wind collide with gas atoms in the atmosphere. The collisions knock the electrons in the atoms into another shell, emitting energy in the form of colored light. These lights can be seen in the skies near the North and South poles and are called auroras.

Heat and light

Bohr's description of electron shells explains how light and other types of radiation are produced by atoms. Light is just one type of electromagnetic radiation. Others include radio waves, heat, ultraviolet light (UV), and x-rays. All these types of radiation are produced in the same way, but some involve greater quantities of energy than others. Visible light lies in the middle of the spectrum—the name given to the range of radiation types. Some rays of light contain more energy than others. Our eyes see these differences as color. Blue light has more energy than yellow light, which has more than red light. UV and x-rays are two examples of radiation that have more energy than visible light. UV is the invisible radiation in sunlight that causes sunburn. X-rays are used to take images of bones inside the body. Heat (or infrared radiation) contains less energy than light, as do radio waves.

Releasing light

Most electromagnetic radiation is released from atoms. When an electron drops down an energy level, the

atom releases a tiny particle called a photon (see illustration on page 20). This particle is even smaller and lighter than an electron. Rays of light or other radiation, such as x-rays, are streams of photons being produced by atoms.

The photon carries the radiation's energy. The amount of energy it carries depends on how many energy levels the electron has dropped. If the electron has moved from a high energy level a long way from the nucleus to a shell near the nucleus, then the photon will carry high-energy radiation such as x-rays. Smaller falls release less energy.

SCIENCE WORDS

- **Energy level:** Electron shells each represent a different energy level. Those closest to the nucleus have the lowest energy.
- **Shell:** The orbit of an electron. Each shell can contain a specific number of electrons and no more.

ELECTRON SHELLS

There is a strict order in which electrons fill the shells that surround the nucleus of an atom. Hydrogen, the first element in the periodic table, has only one electron orbiting its nucleus. Helium, the second element, has two. Because the inner shell is very close to the nucleus, it can hold only two electrons. The next element is lithium, which has three electrons. Since the inner shell is full, the third electron has to orbit in the next shell. The second shell can hold a maximum of eight electrons. Atoms with full outer shells are stable and unreactive. Lithium needs seven electrons and carbon needs four electrons to be stable.

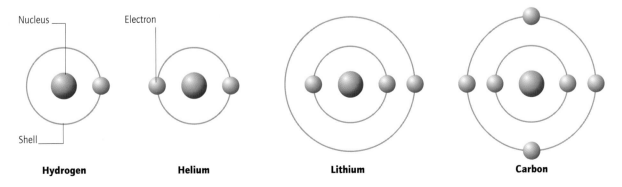

Nucleus   Electron

Shell

Hydrogen   **Helium**   **Lithium**   **Carbon**

Fixed amounts

The energy levels in an atom are fixed. They depend on the atom's size. Electrons can only move between energy levels. They cannot move halfway between two levels. As a result, when they drop down levels, they always release photons with exactly the same amount of energy. This amount of energy is called a quantum. Quanta (the plural of quantum) are fixed amounts of energy. It is not possible for an atom to release half a quantum. This fact forms the basis of quantum physics, the branch of science that investigates the forces that govern atoms.

Because atoms can only release a certain set of fixed amounts of energy, chemists can identify elements by the light they produce. Elements produce light and other radiation when they burn, or when they are heated. Potassium always produces a pale purple flame when it burns, while magnesium burns with a dazzling white flame. Each element produces a characteristic spectrum of colors that identify the element.

PHOTONS

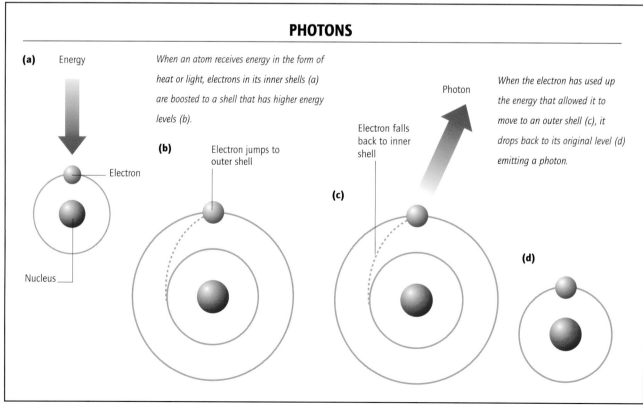

(a) Energy

When an atom receives energy in the form of heat or light, electrons in its inner shells (a) are boosted to a shell that has higher energy levels (b).

Electron

Nucleus

(b) Electron jumps to outer shell

(c) Electron falls back to inner shell

Photon

When the electron has used up the energy that allowed it to move to an outer shell (c), it drops back to its original level (d) emitting a photon.

(d)

The rays of light we see are caused by tiny particles called photons. Photons are created when the electrons that surround atoms change their energy level.

Chemical behavior

Electrons are the parts of an atom that take part in chemical reactions. When atoms join up, they lose, gain, or share their electrons with other atoms. The interaction of electrons creates the forces that hold the atoms together as molecules. Some elements react and form compounds more readily than others. Whether an element is reactive depends on how its electrons are arranged around the nucleus. The arrangement of electrons controls how easy it is for an atom to lose, gain, or share its electrons.

Electron arrangements

The electrons in the outermost shell of an atom are the ones that take part in chemical reactions. Electron shells are most stable when they are completely full. The atoms of most elements have an outer shell that is only partially full. Lithium atoms have just one electron in their second shell, with seven spaces left empty. Chlorine has seven electrons in its outer shell, with room for one more.

Elements take part in chemical reactions that make their outer electron shells more stable. An atom can do

SCIENCE WORDS

- **Electromagnetic radiation:** The energy emitted by a source, for example, x-rays, ultraviolet light, visible light, heat, or radio waves.
- **Photon:** A particle that carries a quantity of energy, usually in the form of light.

FIREWORKS

Fireworks contain small amounts of explosives that blow up to produce a display of colors. The colors in fireworks are produced by certain chemicals mixed into the explosives. When the firework explodes, the atoms in these chemicals react with each other or the air and release energy as colored light.

The color of the light depends on the elements in the firework. If a firework contains potassium compounds, it will explode with a purple color. Lithium atoms produce a red color, while blue sparkles are caused by metals such as copper and cobalt.

The orange color of this firework indicates that it probably contains a sodium salt. Sodium always gives an orange flame when burned.

this by giving away an electron, taking one from another atom, or it can share electrons with another atom so they both have full outer shells. For example, lithium atoms lose their single outer electron during reactions. As a result, the atom also loses its whole second shell, and its first shell becomes the outer one. This shell has two electrons in it and so is full and very stable. On the other hand, chlorine atoms gain an electron when they react. This makes them stable by completing their own outer shell.

REACTIONS AND BONDING

A chemical reaction changes one substance into another. During chemical reactions, atoms join with each other in new ways to form molecules. The molecules are held together by bonds between atoms.

A chemical reaction takes place when two or more substances are mixed together in the right conditions. The substances that are the ingredients needed for the reaction are called the reactants. During the reaction, the atoms inside the reactants separate from each other and reorganize. They form into one or more new substances. Chemists call these substances the products.

Reactants may be elements—with just one type of atom in them—or compounds that are made up of different types of atoms. The products may also be either elements or different compounds. During the reaction, no atoms are made or destroyed. All that happens is that they are rearranged. The number of atoms in the reactants is always the same as the number of atoms in the products.

Chemists show what has happened during a chemical reaction with a chemical equation. Chemical equations have two sides. The left-hand side shows the formulas of the reactants and the number of molecules that are needed for the reaction. The right-hand side shows the formulas of the products and the number of molecules that have been formed.

Coal burning in air is a simple reaction. Coal is mainly pure carbon. The carbon (C) reacts with molecules of oxygen (O_2) in the air. The product of this reaction is carbon dioxide gas (CO_2). The equation for this reaction is:

Carbon + oxygen = carbon dioxide

$$C + O_2 = CO_2$$

One of the most important chemical reactions happens in plants. Plants use energy from the Sun to change water and carbon dioxide into sugars and oxygen.

Breaking and making

The reaction between carbon and oxygen releases a lot of heat and light. Flames are superhot carbon and oxygen atoms in the process of reacting. People have burned coal as a fuel for many centuries because the reaction it produces gives off so much heat.

Other reactions do not produce heat. Instead, these sorts of reactions need to be heated to make them work. When chalky calcium carbonate ($CaCO_3$) is heated it breaks up into calcium oxide (CaO) and carbon dioxide (CO_2). But if the stone is left unheated, the reaction will not take place. The equation for this reaction is:

$$CaCO_3 \rightarrow CaO + CO_2$$

Whether a reaction produces or takes in heat (exothermic or endothermic) depends on the bonds in the reactants and products. These bonds hold the molecules together. During a chemical reaction, some of the bonds in the reactants are broken, and then new bonds form to make the products.

Energy is needed to break a bond, and energy is released when new bonds are formed. When a reaction has finished there is usually a difference between the energy used to break bonds and the energy released as new bonds are made. If more energy is released as the new bonds form than was used to break the old ones, then the reaction releases the spare energy as heat and light. If the new bonds release less energy than was used to break the old bonds, then the reaction needs extra energy to make it happen.

Bonding

Atoms can bond in a number of ways. There are three main types of bonds—ionic, covalent, and metallic. The way particular elements form bonds depends on how many electrons their atoms have in their outer shell. Some elements produce stronger bonds than others.

TRY THIS

Fizzing fun
You can see a quick, safe, and easy chemical reaction for yourself using two common household compounds. Mix a spoonful of baking soda (sodium bicarbonate) with vinegar (ethanoic acid) in a clear glass. When the baking soda is added it begins to fizz. The sodium bicarbonate reacts with the acid to produce three new compounds—sodium ethanoate, water, and carbon dioxide gas. The water and sodium ethanoate form a solution in the glass, while the gas, which causes the fizzing, bubbles away.

Strong bonds need a lot of energy to break them. They are produced when two very reactive atoms bond.

An element's reactivity depends on something called electronegativity. That is a measure of how strongly one atom holds on to its electrons and pulls on the electrons of other atoms. Elements that have an outer electron shell with only a few empty spaces left will pull on electrons the most strongly. Nonmetals are the most electronegative. Fluorine gas is the most electronegative element. It has just one space to fill in its outer shell and so strongly attracts electrons from other atoms. That makes fluorine very likely to react with other elements.

Elements with very low electronegativity are also highly reactive. These elements have just a few electrons in their outer shell. Elements like this are generally metals. Metals do not pull electrons toward them and they hold on to their outer electrons very lightly. This makes them electropositive. The most electropositive elements, such as caesium and francium, have only one electron in their outer shell. When they lose this electron, they become stable.

Ionic bonds

When electronegative and electropositive atoms react they form ionic bonds. An ion is a charged version of an atom. A positively charged ion is an atom that has lost one or more of its electrons. Atoms that gain electrons become negative ions. The size of an ion's charge depends on how many electrons it has lost or gained. For example, chlorine (Cl) atoms gain a single electron to become negative (Cl^-) ions. However, calcium atoms can lose two electrons to become positive (Ca^{2+}) ions.

Charged objects are attracted to objects with an opposite charge. This is the same force that keeps an electron orbiting a nucleus, and pulls ions with opposite charges toward each other. It is this attraction that holds them together, forming an ionic bond.

Sharing electrons

Some elements are neither particularly electropositive nor electronegative. That is because the outer shell is more or less half filled. Such elements have just as many electrons to lose as they have to gain to have a full outer shell. For example, carbon atoms have four electrons in their outer shell. To become stable by having

Antoine Lavoisier

French scientist Antoine Lavoisier (1743-1794) was one of the most important people in modern chemistry—for example, he discovered the element oxygen. But he also did a lot of work to show that atoms were not made or destroyed by chemical reactions, but simply rearranged themselves to form new compounds. Lavoisier carried out many experiments in which he carefully weighed the reactants and then all the products. Each time, his results showed that the amount of matter was always the same after a reaction as before it. The principle he proved is called the law of conservation of mass. Lavoisier came from a noble family in Paris. He inherited a large fortune, but grew even wealthier by collecting taxes from poor French peasants. He used his income to fund his many experiments. After the French Revolution in 1789, Lavoisier was accused of antirevolutionary activities and was imprisoned and guillotined.

IONIC BOND

Common salt (sodium chloride) is a compound held together by an ionic bond. When an ionic bond forms, the single electron in a sodium atom's outer shell breaks free, leaving behind a full outer shell. The sodium atom becomes a positive sodium ion (Na^+). The free electron moves to the chlorine atom. It takes the final place in that atom's outer shell, making the atom a negative chloride ion (Cl^-). The two ions have opposite charges so are attracted to each other. This is the force that bonds them together.

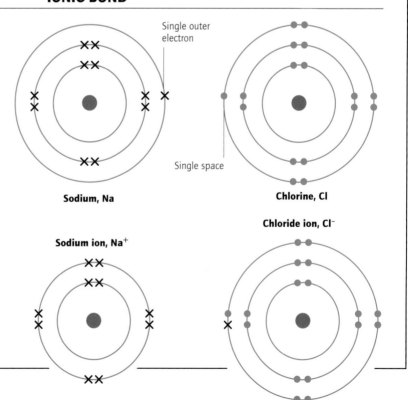

Single outer electron

Single space

Sodium, Na

Chlorine, Cl

Sodium ion, Na⁺

Chloride ion, Cl⁻

a full outer shell, a carbon atom has two options. It can either pull four electrons off other atoms or it can release its four outer electrons. Both are very unlikely because they would require huge amounts of energy.

Instead, carbon and similar elements get a full outer shell by sharing electrons. The shared electrons sit in the outer shells of both atoms. That is called a covalent bond. Each of the shared electrons is being pulled by the nucleus of both atoms. This is the force that holds the atoms together.

Each covalent bond involves two electrons being shared. Some atoms can form more than one covalent bond at a time. A carbon atom, say, can form four covalent bonds at once. These four bonds can be with four other atoms. Sometimes, though, two atoms share two pairs of electrons. These are called double bonds. Carbon can even form triple bonds.

Metallic bonds

Metals are mostly hard solids that can be bent or stretched without breaking. They are also good conductors of heat and electricity. These properties are the result of the way in which a metal's atoms are bonded.

The connections between metals' atoms are called metallic bonds. Metallic bonds involve metal atoms sharing some or all of their outer electrons. Nearly all metallic elements have only one or two outer electrons. Only a few metals, such as lead, bismuth, and tin, have more. When a metal's atoms are packed closely together, as in a solid or liquid, the outer electrons from each atom break free. The free electrons form a "sea" of electrons that can move around and are shared by all the atoms. The positively charged nucleus inside a metal atom is attracted to the negatively charged electron sea all around it. This force holds metal atoms in place.

Intermolecular bonds

Ionic, covalent, and metallic bonds hold atoms together. However, there are other forces that make atoms and molecules cling together.

The atoms in a rubber band are joined in long coiled molecules. These molecules are connected to each other by covalent bonds. When the rubber band is stretched, the long molecules uncoil until the covalent bonds prevent further stretching. Any further tension on the band causes these covalent bonds to break and the band snaps.

Most of these are very weak. For example, tiny temporary forces are produced by the random movement of the electrons. The electrons in an atom or molecule are generally spread out evenly. However, they are all constantly moving and by pure chance they can sometimes all gather in one place at the same time. This gives one end of an atom or molecule a negative charge and the other end becomes positive. These charges exist for only a very short time, but they have an effect by pushing and pulling on the atoms around them.

These forces are named van der Waals forces for Dutch physicist Johannes van der Waals (1837–1923). He was the first to realize the importance of these forces and how they affect the behavior of gases and liquids.

Larger molecules produce stronger van der Waals forces than smaller ones. This increases the melting and boiling points of the larger molecules. Even though they are tiny, the van der Waals forces hold molecules together and make it harder to break the bonds between them.

Dipole attractions

Some types of molecules always have charged ends. These charged regions are called dipoles. Dipoles are produced when one atom in a molecule is more electronegative than the others. As a result, all the outer electrons in the molecule are drawn toward that atom. Because more of the electrons are at one end, that end, or pole, is negative. The other pole is positive. The charged poles are attracted to the oppositely charged pole of a nearby molecule. Dipoles attract the molecules to one another and make them arrange themselves in a repeating pattern, where the oppositely charged poles are next to each other.

Hydrogen bonds

Hydrogen bonds are an example of a dipole attraction. As their name suggests, these bonds always involve an

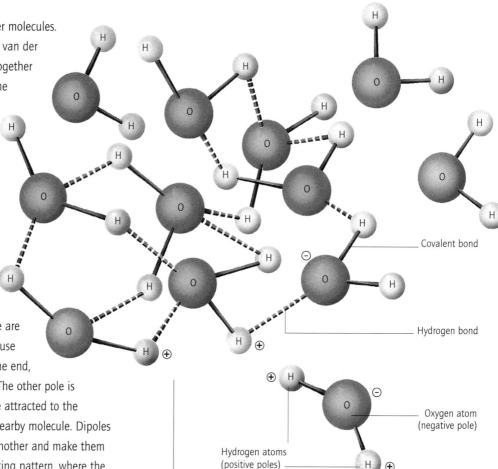

Water (H_2O) molecules form hydrogen bonds. The hydrogen atoms in water have a slight positive charge and the oxygen atoms have a slight negative charge, owing to the arrangement of electrons around each nucleus. These opposite charges attract each other and hold the water molecules loosely together.

---

atom of hydrogen. When hydrogen is bonded to highly electronegative elements, such as fluorine, it often forms a positive pole. The hydrogen atom's only electron is pulled away by the other atom, leaving just the hydrogen's nucleus. This nucleus is a single proton and has a strong positive charge.

Water is an example of a compound that produces hydrogen bonds. The oxygen atom in the water molecule pulls the electrons from the hydrogen atoms. The oxygen has a slightly negative charge, and each

---

SCIENCE WORDS

- **Dipole attraction:** The attractive force between charged ends of molecules.
- **Hydrogen bond:** Dipole attraction that always involves a hydrogen atom.
- **Intermolecular bonds:** The bonds that hold molecules together. These bonds are weaker than those between atoms in a molecule.
- **Van der Waals forces:** Short-lived forces between atoms and molecules.

hydrogen is slightly positive. The positive hydrogen atoms are attracted to the negative pole of another water molecule.

The hydrogen bonds in water ensure that it is a liquid in the normal conditions found on Earth's surface. Without these bonds, water molecules would not be so strongly bonded to each other. As a result, the boiling point of water would be a much lower temperature, and water would be a gas in normal conditions.

Shapes of molecules

As well as sometimes creating weak forces between molecules, the position of electrons in a molecule has an effect on its shape. Opposite charges attract and like charges repel each other. The electrons in a molecule repel each other and they tend to stay as far away from each other as possible. Electrons in an atom's outer shell will repel each other with equal force. However, an electron that is being shared with another atom to form a bond cannot push the other electrons away as strongly. As a result, pairs of shared electrons are often pushed away from the other, unbonded electrons.

The uneven distribution of outer electrons has an effect on the shape of a molecule. A molecule with two atoms, such as a chlorine gas molecule (Cl_2), always forms a straight line and can be thought of as a miniature dumbbell. However, when a molecule has more than one bond in it, the shape can be more complicated.

A molecule of methane gas contains one carbon atom at its center. There are four hydrogen atoms bonded to the carbon. Carbon has four electrons, and each one makes a single covalent bond with one of the hydrogens. Therefore, all pairs of electrons are identical and they all repel each other equally. The result of this is that methane molecules form a tetrahedron—a type of pyramid.

Water molecules, however, are shaped by the force of unbonded electrons. Each molecule is made up of two hydrogen atoms joined to a single oxygen atom by

FLOATING ICE

Water is an unusual substance. Most substances contract a little when they freeze. But water expands when it turns to ice. As a result, ice is less dense than water. This ensures that ponds and rivers always freeze from the top down and makes it possible for huge icebergs to float in the ocean. Ice takes up more room than water because of hydrogen bonds. As water freezes, these bonds force the molecules into a widely spaced crystal structure. When ice melts, hydrogen bonds have less of an effect, the bonds continually break and re-form, and the molecules mingle more closely with each other, taking up less room.

covalent bonds. The molecule is not straight but bent, with both the hydrogen atoms being on the same side of the oxygen atom. That is because the two pairs of shared electrons in the molecule's bonds are being repelled by the oxygen atom's six other electrons.

Atoms can also form molecules that have complex shapes. Carbon atoms can join to make spherical molecules of connected hexagons and pentagons. These molecules are called fullerenes for the American engineer and inventor Buckminster Fuller (1895–1983), who designed domes that have the same structure as these carbon molecules. Carbon can also form sheets of hexagons that roll up to form hollow tubes.

Some elements are unstable. Their atoms break apart and release energy in the form of radiation. This process is called radioactivity.

An atom is described as radioactive if it has an unstable nucleus. An atom's nucleus is made of positively charged protons and neutrally charged neutrons. Particles with the same charge repel each other, and that is true of protons. Yet the protons stay together in the nucleus instead of being forced apart. That happens because there is an even stronger attractive force bonding the protons and neutrons in place. Radioactivity occurs when this strong force cannot keep the nucleus together.

Inside the nucleus of a radioactive atom, the ratio of protons to neutrons makes it hard for the strong force to hold the particles together. Eventually small amounts

Atom bombs make use of the instability of radioactive elements. By exploding these elements, huge quantities of energy are released, along with invisible, but deadly, radiation.

of the nucleus break off and escape from the atom. This process is called radioactive decay. Radioactive decay is a type of nuclear reaction. Nuclear reactions are different from chemical reactions. Chemical reactions involve just the electrons in an atom. Nuclear reactions result in changes to the nucleus of an atom.

Radioactive elements

Radioactive elements are usually those with very large atoms. Their atoms have so many particles in each nucleus that they are more unstable than smaller atoms. For example, uranium atoms have between 234 and 238 particles in their nucleus. Uranium is one of the most common radioactive elements. There are nine other naturally occurring elements with atoms that are

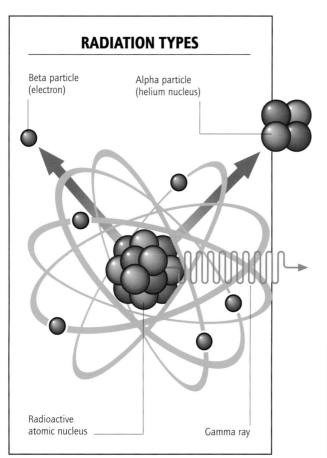

RADIATION TYPES

Beta particle (electron)

Alpha particle (helium nucleus)

Radioactive atomic nucleus

Gamma ray

always radioactive: bismuth, polonium, astatine, radon, francium, radium, actinium, thorium, and protactinium.

However, some isotopes of other elements are radioactive. Isotopes are atoms that have the same atomic number, but have a different atomic mass. One of the rare hydrogen isotopes—tritium—is radioactive. Radioactive isotopes are known as radioisotopes. Radioisotopes are always less common than the stable version of an element. For example, one in every trillion carbon atoms is the radioisotope carbon-14. All the others are stable carbon-12.

Types of radiation

Radioactivity produces three types of radiation (see box opposite). These are alpha particles, beta particles, and gamma rays. Most nuclear reactions release either an alpha particle or a beta particle. All nuclear reactions produce gamma rays.

Alpha particles are two protons and two neutrons stuck together. This is the same as a nucleus of a helium atom, so alpha particles are often written as $^4_2$He. The 4 refers to the atomic mass of the nucleus (how heavy it is) and the 2 refers to the atomic number (the number of protons) of the atom. Because alpha particles do not have any electrons attached to them, the protons they contain give them a positive charge.

Most beta particles are fast-moving electrons. They have a negative charge just like the electrons that orbit

The Curies

Polish physicist Marie Curie (1867–1934) and her French husband Pierre (1859–1906) were pioneers in the study of radioactivity—they even coined the term. Although radiation in the form of x-rays was already known by the time they began work in 1898, nobody really knew where it came from. The Curies discovered that the strength of radiation emitted by a uranium ore depended on the amount of uranium atoms in the compound. Also, after analyzing a mineral called pitchblende, they found it contained uranium compounds that produced more radiation than expected. This suggested that the rock must also contain other radioactive elements, two of which they managed to identify: polonium (named for Marie's homeland) and radium. The Curies were awarded the 1903 Nobel Prize for physics for their work. Marie Curie also won the 1911 Nobel Prize for chemistry for her discovery of radium and polonium.

At the time, the harmful effects of radioactivity were not known, and Marie Curie died of leukemia caused by her exposure to radiation. Her notebooks are still so radioactive that they cannot be handled.

atoms. Beta particles are produced when a neutron in an unstable nucleus breaks down into a proton. A proton is slightly smaller than a neutron, and the leftover matter flies away in the form of an electron.

Gamma rays are energy waves that belong to the electromagnetic spectrum. This spectrum also includes light, heat, radio waves, and x-rays. However, gamma rays contain more energy than any other type of wave. Some nuclear reactions also produce x-rays.

Dangers of radiation

All radiation produced by radioactive substances is dangerous. Alpha and beta particles are charged, and can rip electrons away from other molecules. This process is called ionization.

SCIENCE WORDS

- **Electromagnetic spectrum:** The range of energy waves that includes light, heat, and radio waves.
- **Ionization:** The formation of ions by adding or removing electrons from atoms.
- **Isotopes:** Atoms with the same atomic number, but a different atomic mass.
- **Radiation:** The products of radioactivity— alpha and beta particles and gamma rays.

ANTIMATTER

A few beta particles have a positive charge. They are the same size as electrons, but have an equal and opposite charge. Particles like this are called positrons. Scientists describe particles such as a positron as antimatter. It is exactly the same as a particle of matter—in this case an electron—but has an opposite charge. When matter and antimatter particles meet they are destroyed completely, releasing gamma rays. Positron beta particles are produced when a proton in a nucleus turns into a neutron.

If radiation particles get into a person's body, they can damage the complex molecules inside cells. As a result, important cells may die or go wrong in other ways. For example, sometimes cells go wrong by growing in an uncontrolled way. This unusual growth produces a tumor in the body, which is a type of cancer.

Alpha particles are the largest type of radiation and cause the most damage. They are easy to stop, though, because they cannot pass easily through solid objects. They can be blocked by a sheet of paper or clothing.

Beta particles are much smaller than alpha particles and so can penetrate farther into solid objects. But once they are inside the body, they do less damage than alpha particles because they are so small. Beta particles can be blocked by a thin sheet of metal.

Gamma rays cause ionization inside the body. More penetrating than other types of radiation, they can pass through clothing, metal sheets, and most other everyday objects. Only thick slabs of lead will stop them completely. Yet only a fraction of the gamma rays are absorbed by body tissues and many pass right through the body without having any effect.

Changing elements

After a nucleus has decayed, the number of protons it contains changes. If the nuclear reaction released an alpha particle, there are two fewer protons in the nucleus. If the reaction released a beta particle, one neutron changed into a proton. The nucleus now has one more proton than before. In both cases, the reactions change the atom's atomic number and it becomes a new element. For example, an atom of the most common uranium isotope, U-238, which has the atomic number 92, releases an alpha particle as it decays. It loses two protons and turns into an atom of thorium. That element has the atomic number 90. Thorium is also radioactive. When the thorium atom decays it releases a beta particle. As a result of that type of decay, the atom's nucleus loses a neutron, but gains a proton. That gives it a new atomic number of 91, and the atom has become protactinium.

Decay chain

In the above example of radioactive decay, one radioactive atom decays into another. It may take many nuclear reactions before an atom decays into a stable element and all radioactive behavior comes to an end. Several different elements are produced by the string of nuclear reactions. This is called the decay chain. For example, the decay chain of uranium-238 contains a total

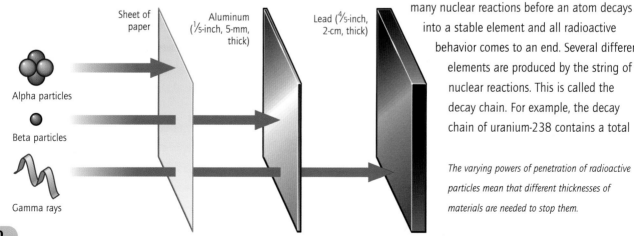

Sheet of paper

Aluminum (1/5-inch, 5-mm, thick)

Lead (4/5-inch, 2-cm, thick)

Alpha particles

Beta particles

Gamma rays

The varying powers of penetration of radioactive particles mean that different thicknesses of materials are needed to stop them.

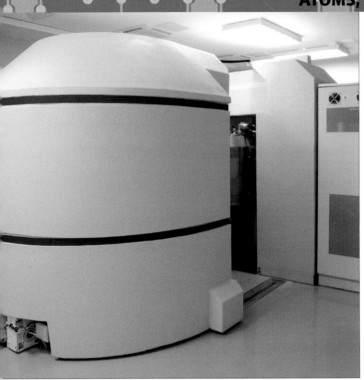

This machine in a medical center is used to produce radionuclides—atoms with unstable nuclei that are used for diagnosis and treatment.

of 14 other isotopes. It eventually ends when stable lead-206 atoms are produced.

The most common naturally occurring radioactive elements on Earth are thorium and uranium. They are found in rocks throughout the world. Most of the other radioactive substances that occur are produced as part of the decay chains of more common elements.

The rarer radioactive elements include radon, the only radioactive element that is a gas, and francium, the most reactive (and rarest) of all metals. The rare elements are more unstable than thorium and uranium and break down quickly.

Half-lives

The rate at which a radioactive element decays is called its half-life. This is the time it takes for half of a sample of radioactive elements to decay. Imagine an element with a half-life of one year. Let us begin with 800 atoms of this element. After the first year only 400 are left. Over the next year, half of the atoms

decay, leaving 200. After the third year, 100 atoms remain. This continues until there are no atoms left.

Common radioactive isotopes are relatively stable and have a very long half-life. For example, thorium-232 has a half-life of 14 billion years. Uranium-238 is less stable, but has a half-life of 4.5 billion years.

The most unstable elements have the shortest half-life. They are extremely rare because they do not exist for long. Even the most stable isotope of francium has a half-life of just 22 minutes. Chemists think that the total amount of francium on Earth adds up to less than 1 ounce (28 g) at any one point in time. Some isotopes are even more unstable and have a half-life of millionths of a second. These isotopes keep undergoing radioactive decay until they reach a stable state.

ARTIFICIAL ELEMENTS

There are 92 naturally occurring elements, 11 of which are radioactive. In addition, some elements, such as carbon, have radioactive isotopes. Scientists have also made artificial elements, all of which are radioactive. They do this by bombarding large natural elements with smaller ions. The atoms are bombarded at such high speed that the ions merge with them into huge artificial atoms.

Most of the artificial elements—26 of which have been made so far—are heavier than uranium. Only 20 of them have names. Many have been named for famous scientists, such as curium (atomic number 96), einsteinium (99), and bohrium (107). Seaborgium (106) was named for American chemist Glenn Seaborg (1912–1999). Seaborg helped make a number of new elements, including plutonium (94), americium (95), berkelium (97), californium (98), and mendelevium (101). These elements all have a very short half-life. For example, the half-life of bohrium is just 10 seconds.

THREE STATES OF MATTER

Everything you can see around you is made of matter, and all of the matter around you exists as a liquid, a solid, or a gas. Matter can change from one form to another.

All matter is made of tiny particles called atoms. When two or more atoms join, they form molecules. Atoms and molecules combine in different ways to form three types of matter—solids, liquids, and gases. These are called states of matter. The states of matter in which a particular substance can exist are called its phases. Water is a type of matter that we are all familiar with. Water commonly exists as a solid phase (ice), a liquid phase (water), and a gas phase (steam).

Solids, liquids, and gases

A solid is matter that has a definite shape and volume (the space that a solid, liquid, or gas occupies). There are two main ways that a solid's particles can be arranged—in neat, ordered rows or randomly. Solids with particles arranged in neat, ordered rows are described as crystalline. Common examples of these are most metals, diamonds, ice, and salt crystals. Solids with particles arranged randomly are described as amorphous. Their texture is usually described as glassy

or rubbery. Common examples are wax, glass, rubber, and plastics. In all solids, the particles are closely packed together, so solids cannot easily be compressed—they cannot be made smaller by squeezing.

Like a solid, a liquid has a definite volume. Unlike a solid, it will take the shape of the container it is poured into. Liquids are described as fluid. A fluid is a substance in which molecules move freely past one another. Like solids, the particles in a liquid are close together. Liquids are also difficult to compress.

Gas is a state of matter that easily changes its shape and volume. Like a liquid, a gas is described as fluid. The particles in a gas quickly spread out to fill all the available space. Because there are large distances between gas particles, gases can easily be compressed to reduce the volume.

SCIENCE WORDS

- **Intermolecular bond:** Weak bond between one molecule and another.
- **Intramolecular bond:** Strong bond between atoms in a molecule.
- **Kinetic energy:** The energy of a moving particle.
- **Kinetic theory:** Theory that describes the properties of matter in terms of the motion of particles.

An image of the Eagle Nebula taken by the Hubble Space Telescope. These brown columns are made from gases and dust, which are in turn made of tiny atoms.

Kinetic theory

Kinetic theory describes the properties of matter in terms of the motion of particles. The particles in all matter are in constant motion. The energy of this motion is called kinetic energy. In solids, the particles are closely packed and their motion limited to vibrations. In a liquid, the particles are usually more widely spaced. They can vibrate but can also move freely throughout the liquid. In a gas, the particles are far apart and move randomly at high speeds.

According to kinetic theory, the faster a particle moves, the more energy it has. We experience this energy as heat. Something with fast-moving particles has a lot of energy and so feels hot. Kinetic theory explains why a hot liquid poured into a cup causes the cup to heat up. The particles in a hot liquid are moving rapidly. As the particles in the liquid strike the surface of the cup, energy passes from the liquid to the cup. The particles in the cup then begin to vibrate. When we pick up a cup, energy from the cup's particles passes to our hand. We feel this energy as heat.

Brownian motion

The movement of molecules in liquids was discovered in 1827 by a Scottish botanist named Robert Brown (1773–1858), who noticed that fresh pollen grains moved randomly in water. By using grains from plants that had been dead for over a century—and noticing that they behaved in exactly the same way, Brown

TRY THIS

Brownian motion

1. Fill a tall glass with water and allow it to sit undisturbed for several hours.

2. Add one or two drops of food coloring to the water and watch how it spreads out. The particles of food coloring spread through the water because of collisions with water molecules. This movement is affected by temperature. If this activity were repeated at a higher temperature, the food coloring would spread more rapidly. At a lower temperature it would spread more slowly.

Add a few drops of food coloring to the water. Make sure the water has been left to settle for a few hours before adding the coloring.

Leave the glass for about 30 minutes. When you come back you will see that the food coloring has spread through the water.

proved that the motion could not come from the grains themselves. This movement, which scientists call Brownian motion in his honor, is now known to result from rapidly moving water molecules colliding with the pollen grains. This is what causes minute particles suspended in a fluid to spread out evenly throughout the fluid. Similar behavior occurs in gases. One example is the spread of a perfume across a room.

BONDING

Two of the strongest intramolecular forces are the ionic and covalent bonds that bind atoms together. Ionic bonds occur when one atom gives one or more electrons to an atom that is trying to fill its outer shell. Covalent bonds are shared between two atoms that both have nearly full shells.

Ionic bonding

Electron

Sodium chloride molecule (NaCl)

Sodium atom

Chlorine atom

Sodium ion

Chloride ion

Covalent bonding

Hydrogen atom

Oxygen atom

Water molecule (H_2O)

Forces within molecules

Atoms are not the smallest pieces of matter. Atoms are made of smaller particles called protons, neutrons, and electrons. The center of an atom is called the nucleus and is made of protons and neutrons. Electrons are arranged around the nucleus in orbits. Electrons and protons both have an electric charge. Electrons have a negative charge and protons have a positive charge. Because their charges are opposite, electrons and protons are attracted to each other. The attractive forces hold electrons in place around the nucleus. These forces also hold atoms together in molecules.

The forces that hold atoms together in molecules are called intramolecular forces. Intra means "within." There are three main types of intramolecular forces. These are covalent bonds, ionic bonds, and metallic bonds. In ionic bonds, one atom gives its electrons to another atom. In covalent bonds, atoms share electrons. In

metallic bonds, electrons move freely among atoms.

The forces that work between molecules are called intermolecular forces. These are the forces that determine whether a substance is a solid, liquid, or gas.

Forces between molecules

Intermolecular forces hold molecules together. Inter means "between" or "among." Compared with intramolecular forces, intermolecular forces are weak. In fact, intermolecular forces are typically only about 15 percent of the strength of intramolecular forces. There are three main types of intermolecular forces. These are the dipole–dipole forces, the London dispersion forces, and hydrogen bonding forces. All of these attractions involve partial electric charges. The charges result from the arrangement of electrons and nuclei in the molecule. Sometimes the arrangement of electrons leaves the nucleus partially exposed, resulting in a small positive charge. At the same time, the electrons are bunched together, producing a small negative charge. It is the attraction between these charges that holds molecules together.

When a substance boils, the particles in it have enough kinetic energy to overcome the intermolecular forces. Boiling is a process by which particles gain enough energy to jump out of a liquid and become a gas. The kinetic energy to make this possible comes from the heat applied to the liquid. Substances with higher boiling points have stronger intermolecular forces than substances with lower boiling points.

Hydrogen bonding

Hydrogen bonds are a strong form of intermolecular bond. Water molecules are held together by these bonds. Water molecules have a neutral charge overall—their number of electrons balances their number of protons. However, water molecules have partial charges at specific locations on the molecule that are strongly attracted to the opposite charge on another water molecule. As a result, water molecules need a bigger input of energy to provide them with enough kinetic energy to overcome the force of the hydrogen bonds. Water therefore has an unusually high boiling point.

Water's high boiling point is not its only unusual property. Ice (solid water) is one of the

few solid phases that floats in its liquid phase. This is because when it becomes a solid, the hydrogen bonds hold the water molecules apart rather than allow them to get closer together, as in other solids. This gives ice a lower density than water, so it floats. Ice does not have a much lower density than water so only a small portion of ice sticks out of the water, as seen in icebergs.

Changing states

When heat is added to a solid, its atoms vibrate more rapidly and its temperature increases. At a certain temperature, a solid will begin to melt. As more energy is added to the solid its temperature does not increase, but more of the solid melts. Eventually all of the solid will have melted and become a liquid—it will have changed state from solid to liquid. Now if more energy is added, the temperature of the liquid will increase. Similarly, at a certain temperature, the liquid will begin to turn into a gas. As more energy is added to the liquid, its temperature does not increase, but more of the liquid becomes a gas. Eventually all of the liquid will become a gas. Now if more energy is added, the temperature of the gas will increase.

Plasma is usually considered to be a fourth state of matter. Plasmas consist of freely moving charged particles, such as electrons, and particles called ions, which are atoms that have lost or gained one or more electrons. Plasmas are formed when the electrons are stripped away from atoms. A fun way of seeing the effect of this state of matter is a plasma globe.

Gases are substances that are constantly moving. They have properties that are affected by heat and pressure, which makes them very useful in many different applications.

You are surrounded by gases. Solids and liquids are easy to see, but gases are usually not visible. The first gas to be studied, more than 300 years ago, was air. Air is all around us, but at the outset scientists did not know that it is composed of many different gases. One of their most surprising discoveries was that, despite being a mixture, air still behaves the same way as a pure gas. In fact, gases all behave in a similar manner regardless of whether they are composed of single atoms, paired atoms, or molecules made up of many types of atoms. Because of this common behavior, the rules applying to any one gas also apply to all other types.

When gases are compared with each other, they are compared at the same temperature and pressure. The standard used to compare gases is called Standard Temperature and Pressure, or STP. In STP, temperature is measured using the Celsius scale or the Kelvin scale. Pressure is measured in units called atmospheres. STP is defined as 0°C (or 273K, –32°F) and 1 atmosphere of pressure. When doing calculations involving gases and temperatures, scientists use the Kelvin scale. Zero on the Kelvin scale is the coldest temperature theoretically possible in the universe (–273°C; –459°F).

Chemists often compare gases by using a type of unit called a mole. A mole of any substance contains 602,213,670,000,000,000,000,000 (6.022×10^{23}) atoms or molecules. At STP, 1 mole of any gas has a volume of 3 cubic feet (22.4 l).

Physical properties of gases

All gases share a set of physical properties. The following six properties are common to all gases:

1. All gases have mass. Mass is a measure of the amount of matter something contains. A helium-filled balloon has mass, but it floats because its mass is less than that of the gases in the surrounding air.

2. Gases are easily compressed (i.e. squeezed into a smaller volume, as with the compressed air in a car tire). Solids and liquids are not easily compressed.

3. Gases spread out to fill the available space. When in a container, gases spread out until they are evenly distributed within that container. When you blow up a balloon, the inside of the balloon has air distributed throughout the balloon. The air will not concentrate in any one part of the balloon.

4. Different gases move through each other easily. The movement of one gas through another is called

Balloons filled with helium gas. Helium atoms have less mass per unit of volume than most other gases. That makes them lighter than the surrounding air, so balloons containing helium float upward.

diffusion. Diffusion occurs because of the random motion of the gas particles colliding with each other. Eventually the gas particles become evenly spread out. Diffusion explains why air is a mixture of gases.

5. Gases exert pressure. The air in car tires is under pressure. You may have also experienced a pressure change when in a car, plane, or elevator. When going up rapidly, you may have felt your ears "pop." That happens because the ears need to maintain a constant pressure to protect your eardrums.

6. The pressure of a gas depends on its temperature. When the temperature is high, gas pressure increases and when it is low, the pressure decreases. In places with very hot summers, car tires can become dangerously overinflated. In places with cold winters, the opposite happens.

These six gas properties are all explained by the kinetic molecular theory. Using this theory, scientists can construct a model that explains each of these behaviors for any gas.

Kinetic theory of gases

The kinetic theory can explain all six of the properties of a gas. You have already read that gas particles have higher kinetic energy than particles in solids or liquids. Gas particles are always colliding with each other. One way to imagine a container of gas is to think of a large jar filled with small rubber balls. As you shake the jar, the rubber balls bounce off each other and the walls of the jar. However, gas particles have their own kinetic energy so the container does not need to be shaken.

These collisions of gas particles are described as elastic collisions. An elastic collision means that no energy is lost in the collision. Rubber balls do not have elastic collisions. When you drop a rubber ball it bounces, but each bounce is lower than the previous

TRY THIS

Bubbles float or sink?

1 Make a hole in the lid of a bottle just big enough to fit some rubber tubing into it. Ask an adult to help.
2 Mix a small amount of dish soap with water in a bowl.
3 Dip a bubble wand into the soapy water, remove it, and wave the wand in the air. The bubbles should float.
4 Add a small amount of baking soda, water, and vinegar to the bottle and put the lid on. This reaction produces carbon dioxide.
5 Dip the bubble wand into the soapy water and hold it close to the end of the rubber tubing. There should be enough carbon dioxide coming out of the tube to blow bubbles. Observe the bubbles of carbon dioxide. They should drop to the ground. That is because carbon dioxide is heavier than air.

Carbon dioxide exits the tube and "blows a bubble." The bubble sinks because carbon dioxide is heavier than air.

bounce because some of the energy is transferred to the surface during each bounce. If a rubber ball could have a perfectly elastic bounce, it would continue bouncing back to exactly the same height.

Because gas particles have kinetic energy, they strike the walls of their container, which creates

DIFFUSION AND EFFUSION

Sometimes gas particles are so small that they pass through the space between molecules, for example in a balloon, a single particle at a time. This process is related to diffusion, but it is called effusion. These artworks illustrate the how effusion affects balloons that have been filled with different gases.

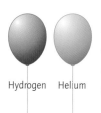

Hydrogen and helium balloons float because they are lighter than air. The balloon of oxygen is heavier than air and does not float.

Hydrogen   Helium

Oxygen

Hydrogen atoms are light and fast moving, so this balloon will deflate first.

Helium atoms are slightly heavier than hydrogen, so this balloon will deflate less quickly.

Oxygen atoms are larger and slower than the two other gases, so this balloon will be the last to deflate.

The rate at which a gas can escape by effusion depends on its molecular mass and how fast the molecules are moving. Lighter and faster-moving gases will effuse more quickly than slow, heavy ones.

pressure. One of the properties of gases is that as temperature increases, pressure increases. That is explained by the fact that at higher temperatures, the gas particles are moving faster, so there are more collisions with the wall of the container.

The kinetic theory of gases can be summarized in four statements:

1. A gas consists of molecules in constant random motion.

2. Gas molecules influence each other only by collision; they exert no other forces on each other.

3. All collisions between gas molecules are perfectly elastic; all kinetic energy is conserved—the total amount of kinetic energy in the gas remains the same.

4. The volume occupied by the molecules of a gas is very small; the vast majority of a gas's volume is empty space through which the gas molecules are moving.

Measuring gases

Four variables are used to describe a gas, and to predict how a gas will behave when conditions are changed. The four variables are volume, temperature, pressure, and the number of gas molecules.

The amount of gas (n) is the quantity of gas expressed in moles. The amount of gas in the sample being measured is found by dividing the mass (in grams) of the gas by the mass of one mole of the gas (in grams per mole).

The volume (V) of a gas is the size of the container. The volume of gases is usually measured in liters (l).

The temperature (T) is usually measured with a thermometer. Scientists use thermometers that measure temperature in degrees Celsius (°C). Calculations involving gases use the Kelvin (K) scale to measure temperature. Adding 273 to the temperature in degrees Celsius gives the temperature in Kelvin. The pressure (P) is the measure of the number of collisions by particles with the wall of the container. Because the particles strike all surfaces of the container, the pressure is the outward force of the particles pushing against the interior surface of the container.

changed. His experiments showed there was a mathematical relationship between the pressure and volume. He expressed this relationship with the following equation:

$$P_1 V_1 = P_2 V_2$$

The equation tells us that the initial pressure of the gas (P_1) multiplied by its initial volume (V_1) is equal to the final pressure of the gas (P_2) multiplied by its final volume (V_2).

According to this equation, if pressure increases, then volume decreases. In turn, if pressure decreases, the volume increases. Because the values change in opposite directions, this is called an inverse relationship.

Charles's law

The 18th-century French chemist, physicist, and aeronaut Jacques Charles (1746–1823) was also interested in gases. His work centered on the relationship between temperature and volume of a gas. He designed an experimental device that trapped a gas with a movable piston. He could heat or cool the container and measure how much the piston moved as the temperature changed. By finding how much the

The deeper divers go, the greater the pressure. This pressure is a major concern, because it forces nitrogen gas in the blood to dissolve. If divers ascend too quickly, the sudden release of pressure forms nitrogen bubbles in their blood ("the bends"), which can be fatal.

The gas laws

When scientists started studying gases in the 17th and 18th centuries, they found that all gases behaved similarly when certain conditions changed. These observations and experiments eventually led to a number of scientific laws that describe the behavior of gases. These scientific laws are called the gas laws. The gas laws can be expressed mathematically using the variables of quantity of gas, volume, temperature, and pressure.

Boyle's law

In the 17th century, an English chemist and physicist named Robert Boyle (1627–1691) noticed that air could be compressed. He performed a series of experiments with air sealed in a tube. By increasing or decreasing the pressure, he found that the volume

TRY THIS

Shrinking balloon
1 Blow up a balloon.
2. Place the balloon in the freezer for about 30 minutes.
3 Remove the balloon from the freezer. How does the size of the balloon compare with when it was placed in the freezer?

What do you think will happen as the balloon warms up? Watch and find out. The balloon changes size because the molecules slow down as the temperature decreases and speed up as the temperature increases.

piston moved, he could calculate the change in the volume of the gas at the different temperatures. He expressed this relationship with the following equation:

$$V_1/T_1 = V_2/T_2$$

This equation tells us that the initial volume (V_1) divided by the initial temperature (T_1) is equal to the final volume (V_2) divided by the final temperature (T_2).

According to this equation, if the temperature increases, the volume also increases. Conversely, if the temperature decreases, the volume also decreases. Because the values change in the same direction, this is called a direct relationship. In the shrinking balloon activity, this relationship is shown by comparing the balloon before and after it is placed in the freezer.

Avogadro's law

In the early 19th century, the Italian chemist Amedeo Avogadro (1776–1856) suggested a simple yet profound relationship between the number of particles of gas and its volume. This relationship states that

SCIENCE WORDS

- **Compress:** To reduce in size or volume by squeezing or exerting pressure.
- **Gas:** A substance such as air that spreads out to fill the available space.
- **Mole:** The amount of any substance that contains the same number of atoms or molecules as 12 grams of carbon. This number is called the Avogadro number and equals 6.022×10^{23}.
- **Pressure:** The force produced by pressing on something.
- **Temperature:** A measure of the hotness or coldness of a substance.
- **Volume:** The space that a solid, liquid, or gas occupies.

CHARLES'S LAW

Charles's experiment with a movable piston is designed to show how heating a gas can change its volume. At room temperature, the piston remains at the same level. When heat is applied to the container, the gas molecules become more energetic and start to exert pressure on the piston, forcing it upward. When the heat is removed, the piston sinks as the gas loses energy and cools.

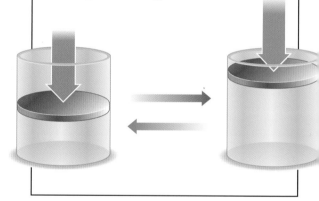

equal volumes of gases at the same temperature and pressure contain an equal number of particles.

Later, scientists proved that Avogadro's hypothesis was correct. Experiments have shown that 1 mole of any gas at STP occupies 22.4 liters. Avogadro's law is expressed with the following mathematical equation:

$$V_1/n_1 = V_2/n_2$$

This equation shows that the initial volume of a gas (V_1) divided by the initial number of moles (n_1) is equal to the final volume of the gas (V_2) divided by the final number of moles (n_2). Put more simply, if the volume of a gas increases, the number of moles increases proportionally. This is true only if the temperature and pressure of the gas remain the same throughout the experiment. The equation shows a direct relationship because as volume increases, the number of moles increases, too.

The ideal gas law

The three gas laws all relate to certain variables that describe gases. These gas laws can be combined in one equation called the ideal gas law. This combines the proportionalities expressed in each equation. When combined, the ideal gas law is stated as:

$$PV = nRT$$

You have seen four of these quantities described in detail already. The only new one is the constant R. The constant R is called the gas constant. The value of the gas constant is $8.314 \text{ Jmol}^{-1}\text{K}^{-1}$. The units in this constant are energy in joules (J) per mole (mol^{-1}) per degree Kelvin (K^{-1}). This constant represents the conditions of a gas at STP.

Chemists call this the ideal gas law because it describes the behavior of an ideal gas in terms of pressure, volume, temperature, and moles. An ideal gas to a chemist is one described by the kinetic theory. While there is really no such thing as an ideal gas, it does describe the behavior of real gases under conditions near to STP. At very low temperatures, gases do not behave as ideal gases.

The atmosphere

Gas pressure is measured in units called atmospheres. The instrument used to measure air pressure is the barometer. Air pressure is caused by the pull of gravity on the gases in the atmosphere.

Air pressure varies with changes in the weather. Air pressure also changes with elevation. As elevation increases, air pressure decreases. The air pressure decreases about 1 inch of mercury for every 1,000-foot rise, or 1 millibar for each 8-meter rise. So, in a jet airliner cruising at 35,000 feet (10,600 m), the air pressure outside the plane is only $\frac{1}{20}$ of the pressure at sea level.

The higher you climb above sea level, the lower the atmospheric pressure becomes. At the top of Mount Everest the atmosphere is very thin. Mountaineers carry oxygen supplies with them because there are not enough oxygen molecules at this level. Also, the atmospheric pressure is too low to make the air flow easily into their lungs.

Liquids are an interesting state of matter with many unusual properties. They have no shape of their own and cannot be squashed or stretched. Liquids can be thick or runny. Water is the most unusual liquid of all.

Liquids take the shape of whatever container they are put in. But the volume of the liquid does not change with the size or shape of the container. So, liquids have a definite volume, unlike gases, but they can change shape. In gases, the particles are far enough apart and have enough kinetic energy to change volume. In liquids, the particles are much closer together and they have forces that attract the particles to each other. Even so, they have enough kinetic energy to slide past each other. The ability to move in this way is what allows a liquid to take the shape of its container.

Compounds that are liquids at room temperature and a pressure of 1 atmosphere are made of molecules. These molecules have varying intermolecular forces that affect how close the molecules are to each other and how they interact. The strength of the intermolecular forces also affects certain physical properties of the liquid.

Physical properties

If you have ever tried to pour honey, you know that it pours very slowly compared to water. Honey is very thick. The term used to describe how a liquid pours is viscosity, defined as a liquid's resistance to flow. Honey has a high viscosity and water has a low viscosity. So, while water flows freely, honey does not. The intermolecular forces in a liquid cause viscosity. If these forces are strong, the molecules do not slide past each other easily and the viscosity is high.

Viscosity is also affected by temperature. At higher temperatures, the molecules have more energy. Because they have more energy, the molecules are able to overcome some of the intermolecular forces and move more easily. This reduces viscosity. Likewise, when the

Honey is a thick and sticky liquid with a high viscosity. This viscosity is what makes honey slow to flow off a spoon or ladle.

temperature is low, the viscosity increases because the molecules have less energy.

Water has hydrogen bonds that act as strong intermolecular forces. Even though water pours more easily than honey, it is still fairly viscous for its molecular size. By comparison, rubbing alcohol has a very low viscosity. If you pour equal amounts of water and rubbing alcohol onto a surface, the rubbing alcohol spreads out more quickly than the water.

Another property of liquids is called surface tension. You may have seen an insect called a water strider skate on the surface of water. The water strider is held up by the surface tension of the water. Uneven forces cause surface tension at the surface of a liquid. The uneven forces cause the surface of the liquid to act like a film. Water has a rather high surface tension. To demonstrate the strength of surface tension, try floating a needle on the surface of water.

Surface tension also explains why water beads up on a surface, such as scattered raindrops on a window pane. The water drops take on a circular shape as this minimizes the surface area.

Surface tension is related to viscosity. Liquids with a high viscosity have a high surface tension. A drop of honey on a plate will hold its circular shape. But if you place a drop of rubbing alcohol on a plate, it will spread out over a large area. The rubbing alcohol has a low surface tension because the intermolecular forces between molecules are low.

Like viscosity, surface tension is affected by temperature. At a lower temperature, the surface tension is greater because molecules have less kinetic energy and so it is more difficult for them to overcome the intermolecular forces. At a higher temperature, the molecules have more kinetic energy so they create less surface tension.

Adding another substance to the liquid may also reduce surface tension. Soap is used to reduce the surface tension of water. If you repeat the floating needle activity, you can add a drop of dish soap to the bowl of water and the needle will immediately sink.

The strangeness of water

Water is the most common liquid on Earth. It is in the oceans, in the atmosphere, and in rivers, lakes, and glaciers. All living organisms need water, and it forms a large part of their bodies. In fact, the human body is about 60 percent water. But for all its familiarity, water has many special and unusual properties.

You have already read that the solid form of water floats in the liquid form. This rare property is important in nature. When a lake freezes, the surface ices over. The ice blanket insulates the water below from the freezing temperatures above. This allows plants and animals in the water to survive.

Water also has a high boiling point for a compound with its molecular size. Other compounds with a similar

TRY THIS

Floating needle

1 Fill a bowl with water.

2 Hold a sewing needle horizontally with some tweezers.

3 Slowly lower the needle to the surface of the water.

4 When the needle is horizontal with and touching the water's surface, release the needle. The needle should float on the surface of the water. It may take several times before you get the needle to float. The needle floats because water has a very high surface tension and is able to support the mass of the needle.

SURFACE TENSION

The surface tension of a liquid is a result of the forces between molecules. In the body of the liquid, molecules are surrounded on all sides, so the forces they exert are even in all directions. On the surface, the molecules have no other liquid molecules above them so the horizontal forces between their nearest neighbors become stronger, forming a firm surface layer.

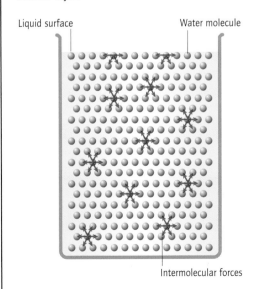

Liquid surface   Water molecule

Intermolecular forces

size such as ammonia (NH_3) and hydrogen sulfide (H_2S) are all gases at room temperature.

Water absorbs a large amount of heat for its volume. The large heat capacity of water helps moderate the overall temperature of Earth by resisting huge temperature changes between day and night by absorbing and releasing heat.

Water turns into a gas only at high temperatures. It takes lots of energy to turn water from a liquid to a gas.

The high surface tension of water leads to a phenomenon called capillary action. Because of the unequal forces at the surface of water, water will rise in a narrow tube.

RAINDROPS

People often describe raindrops as teardrop shaped. But when raindrops fall from the sky, they are not shaped like that. Water has a high surface tension, and that tends to pull all the molecules together when in a drop. This makes a water drop spherical in shape, because all the surface forces are equal in a sphere. As a raindrop falls, its bottom surface flattens slightly as a result of air resistance, but the top of the drop remains rounded.

Raindrops are usually between $^4/_{1000}$ and $^1/_5$ inch (0.1-5 mm) in diameter, but can reach $^1/_3$ inch (8 mm). If raindrops grow larger than this, air resistance causes them to break up into smaller drops.

This high-speed photograph of raindrops shows that they are not shaped like teardrops, but are almost spherical.

Water reaches the leaves at the top of a tree by an effect called capillary action.

Liquid to gas

When enough heat is added to a liquid, it begins to boil and turn into a gas. This temperature is called the boiling point. Adding heat to a liquid gives the molecules in the liquid more kinetic energy. When they get enough kinetic energy, they can escape the intermolecular forces of the liquid and become a gas. The process of a liquid changing into a gas is also called vaporization. Vaporization describes boiling and it also describes evaporation.

If you have ever left a glass of water sitting out for a long period of time, you may have noticed that the volume decreases. Some of the water molecules have escaped from the liquid and become gas. The term for this is evaporation. When a liquid evaporates, it changes to a gas without boiling. Temperature is a measure of the average kinetic energy. In reality, some molecules have more energy than average and others have less. Some of the molecules with more kinetic energy have enough energy to overcome intermolecular forces and escape the liquid to become a gas. As temperature increases, evaporation increases since more molecules have enough energy to escape the liquid.

If you place some water in a container and pump out the excess air, the liquid will evaporate until the pressure of the liquid and its vapor are in equilibrium. The pressure of the vapor at this point is called the liquid's vapor pressure. At the same time as some water molecules evaporate, some of the molecules in the vapor condense or return to the liquid. In equilibrium, the rate of evaporation and the rate of condensation are equal.

All liquids create a vapor. In liquids with low intermolecular forces, evaporation occurs more readily. For example, alcohol evaporates much more quickly than water because the molecules do not need as much energy to escape the liquid.

Boiling point

When you heat a pan of water, tiny bubbles form on the bottom of the pan, which reaches boiling point first. These bubbles are water vapor. As more heat is added more of the water reaches boiling point and the bubbles grow larger. Soon, lots of bubbles are rising to the surface quickly. When this happens, you know the water is boiling. Sometimes small bubbles appear even before the bottom of the pan has reached boiling point. These are actually air bubbles resulting from air that was dissolved in the water, since the solubility of air in water goes down as the temperature increases.

Boiling an egg on a mountain top takes longer than at sea level. The reason for this is that atmospheric pressure is lower at high altitude. Remember that water boils when the vapor pressure is equal to the atmospheric pressure. At high altitude, the atmospheric pressure is lower so the temperature at which water boils is also lower. In fact, if you lower the pressure enough, water will boil at room temperature.

TRY THIS

Cloud in a jar
Water vapor is a colorless gas. However, if it cools quickly, it can form tiny droplets that appear white as they scatter light. That is what happens in the vapor trails you see behind jets.

1 Pour about ¼ cup (60 ml) of water into a jar.

2 Turn a rubber glove inside out. Place a floating candle inside the jar and ask an adult to light it. After a few seconds, blow it out and quickly stretch the glove completely over the mouth of the jar.

3 Put your hand inside the glove and push your hand into the jar. Take care not to touch the candle—it may still be hot.

4 Carefully bend your fingers into a fist and pull up while holding the jar steady. You should see a cloud form in the jar. The cloud will disappear when you stop pulling up. The cloud forms because the change in pressure causes some of the water vapor to condense (change back to a liquid) and become visible.

SOLUTIONS

Substances are rarely pure. Most of the time they are mixed in different ways. A solution is one type of mixture. A cup of coffee, a steel bar, and even the air are examples of solutions. Other mixtures include suspensions and colloids.

There are two basic types of mixtures: homogeneous and heterogeneous mixtures. In a heterogeneous mixture, all the ingredients are still identifiable and they can be separated from each other relatively easily. In a homogeneous mixture, the substances included are mixed evenly so you cannot see one from another. Seawater is a homogeneous mixture. It is not possible to see the water, salts, and other things mixed into it. A bowl of noodle soup is a heterogeneous mixture. You can see the broth, noodles, and other ingredients.

A solution is the most common type of homogeneous mixture. A solution is a homogeneous mixture that is in a single physical state. The most

SCIENCE WORDS

- **Heterogeneous mixture:** A mixture in which ingredients are not spread evenly.
- **Homogeneous mixture:** A mixture in which substances are spread out evenly.
- **Insoluble:** When a substance will not dissolve in another substance.
- **Soluble:** When a substance can dissolve in another substance.
- **Solute:** A substance that is dissolved to form a solution.
- **Solution:** A homogeneous mixture where substances are in the same physical state.
- **Solvent:** A substance in which a solute is dissolved.

A tablet dissolves in water. As it does, the tablet breaks up into its smallest units and spreads throughout the water.

familiar solutions, such as seawater or soda, are liquids. Solutions can also be gases or solids. The air is a solution of gases, while bronze (which is a mixture of copper and tin) is a solid solution.

Properties of solutions

To have a solution, there must be one or more substances dissolved into another substance. The substance that is dissolved is called a solute. The substance that the solute is dissolved into is called the solvent. For example, if you add a spoonful of table salt to a glass of water, you make a solution. The table salt dissolves in the water, so the salt is the solute. The water is the solvent.

Not every substance will dissolve in every other substance. You may have heard the expression "oil and water do not mix." You can demonstrate this by adding oil to water. If a solute does not dissolve in solvent, it is called insoluble. If a solute does dissolve in a solvent, it is described as soluble.

Types of solutions

Most people think of solutions as liquids, but that does not have to be the case. Solutions can be any combination of solutes and solvents in different states.

Solid solutions generally involve at least one metal. For example, sterling silver has a small amount of copper mixed into it. The copper is the solute and the silver is the solvent. Gold used for jewelry also has copper dissolved in it, and steel is made by dissolving a small amount of carbon in iron. Solid solutions including metals are called alloys. Alloys are made by mixing the metals while they are melted into liquids.

Solutions of gases are homogeneous mixtures of two or more gases. An example of a gaseous solution is the air all around us. Air is composed of mainly oxygen and nitrogen. Most of it is nitrogen—78 percent—so that is the solvent. Oxygen makes up 21 percent of the air, so it is the main solute. The air also contains several other gas solutes, including argon and carbon dioxide.

TRY THIS

Colorful solutions

You can watch a solid dissolving in a liquid with this simple activity. You will need a tall, clear drinking glass, a powdered fruit drink, and a flat toothpick. Select a fruit drink with a dark color, such as grape or cherry.

1 Fill the glass with water.
2 Use the wide, flat end of the toothpick to pick up a small amount of the fruit powder.
3 Gently shake the crystals of powder into the water in the glass.
4 Observe the crystals of the powder as they fall into the glass.

The tiny grains of powdered fruit drink are the solute. You can see them dissolve in the water because they create a colored solution. The color will spread out from the crystals and eventually fill the whole glass. This occurs due to a process called diffusion. Diffusion makes a liquid or gas spread out. This results from the random motion of the molecules making up the gas or liquid, as in Brownian motion (see page 33).

Liquid solutions must have a liquid solvent, but they can involve a solid, liquid, or gas as a solute. For example, river water has oxygen dissolved in it. Fish and other underwater creatures depend on this oxygen for their survival. Solids can form solutions with liquids, too. For example, a sugar lump will dissolve in warm water.

Liquids that dissolve liquids are less common. One example is the antifreeze added to the water in a car's radiator. The water dissolves in the antifreeze, which prevents the water from freezing.

Liquids that mix easily, like antifreeze and water, are said to be miscible. Other liquids, such as oil and water, do not mix at all. Liquids that do not mix are described as immiscible.

Tea is a solution that forms when chemicals in dried tea leaves dissolve in hot water. Strong tea has a higher concentration of these chemicals than weak tea.

Dissolving in water

Water is sometimes called the universal solvent because it can dissolve so many different substances. The solutions it forms are described as aqueous solutions, from *aqua*, the Latin word for "water."

A solute that dissolves in water either forms ions or molecules. An ion is an atom that has lost or gained one or more electrons. As a result, the ion has a charge. An ion that has lost electrons has a positive charge, while one that has gained an electron is negatively charged. A molecule is a collection of two or more atoms that are connected by chemical bonds. Molecules do not have a charge.

Ions are attracted to other ions that have an opposite charge. They are repelled by ions with the same charge. The attraction makes ions combine to form compounds. Compounds are substances that contain the atoms of two or more elements joined together by chemical bonds. An ionic compound always contains both positive and negative ions. When these compounds dissolve in water, the ions separate.

Table salt (sodium chloride) is an example of an ionic compound. It is made from positively charged sodium ions and negatively charged chloride ions. When dissolved in water, it splits into sodium and chloride ions.

Molecular compounds, such as sugar, are formed when atoms share their electrons. They also break up when they dissolve. However, they separate into uncharged molecules.

Carrying currents

Because they are charged, dissolved ions will carry an electric current through a solution. For this reason, ionic solutions are a type of electrolyte—a liquid that carries electricity. Molecular solutions contain no charged particles, so they do not conduct electric currents.

Concentration

The amount of solute in a given quantity of solvent is measured as the concentration. Knowing the concentration is useful. It allows chemists to compare solutions or to mix substances in a precise way.

Concentration is measured in many different ways. Chemists can express concentration in three ways molarity, molality, and mole fraction.

Molarity (M) is the most common way chemists express concentration. The molarity of solution is defined as the number of moles of solute in a liter (0.26 gallons) of solvent. One mole contains

SCIENCE WORDS

- **Compound:** A substance that contains two or more elements joined together by chemical bonds.
- **Electrolyte:** An ionic substance that can conduct electricity.
- **Electron:** A negatively charged particle that orbits an atom's nucleus.
- **Immiscible:** When substances cannot mix.
- **Ion:** An atom that has lost or gained an electron or electrons.
- **Miscible:** When substances can mix.
- **Molecule:** A collection of two or more atoms that are connected by bonds.

602,213,670,000,000,000,000,000 (6.022×10^{23}) atoms or molecules. To calculate molarity, you find the number of moles of the solute and divide by the number of liters of solution.

Molality is a similar measure of concentration. Molality (m) is the number of moles of solute dissolved in a kilogram (2.2 pounds) of solvent. Molality is more accurate than molarity in some ways. As a liquid changes temperature, the volume will also change slightly. Molality is based on the mass of the solvent, not its volume, so it is the same whatever the temperature. Molarity is based on volume and will change slightly with temperature.

Mole fraction is a third way to measure concentration. It is the ratio of the number of moles of one substance in a solution to the total number of moles of all the substances in the solution. Adding all the fractions together always equals 1. The mole fraction is not affected by the temperature of the solution.

Saturation and solubility

When a solute is added to a solution, only so much of it can dissolve in the solvent. When the maximum amount of solute has dissolved, the solution is said to be saturated. If you add several spoonfuls of sugar to a glass of warm water, some of the sugar will not dissolve in the water no matter how hard you stir. The water has become saturated with sugar, and the remaining sugar stays in the bottom of the glass.

Solubility is defined as the amount of a solute that will dissolve in a solvent under a given set of conditions. A substance's solubility changes as these conditions change. For example, you can dissolve more sugar in hot water than in cold.

Factors affecting solubility

A substance's solubility is determined by the nature of the solute and the solvent. For example, solutes and solvents are either polar or nonpolar. Molecules that are polar have small electric charges at certain locations. These locations are known as poles—like the

TRY THIS

Making ice cream

Ice cream is a solution of frozen milk and flavorings. To make ice cream you will need 2 cups (480 ml) of milk, ¼ cup (50 g) of sugar, 2 teaspoons of vanilla extract, 4 cups (960 ml) of ice, ½ cup (100 g) of salt, 2 Ziploc bags—one large and one small, and some duct tape.

1 Add the milk, sugar, and vanilla to the small Ziploc bag and tape it shut. Shake the bag to mix.
2 Mix the ice cubes and salt together in the large Ziploc bag.
3 Push the small Ziploc bag into the ice in the large Ziploc bag so it is surrounded with as much ice as possible.
4 Shake the large Ziploc bag up and down and back and forth for 15 minutes.
5 Remove the small Ziploc bag and enjoy your ice cream.

The salt lowers the temperature of the ice in the large bag. The ice becomes cold enough to freeze the mixture of milk and sugar to make ice cream.

SCIENCE WORDS

- **Saturated:** A solution that has the maximum amount of solute dissolved in the solvent.
- **Solubility:** A measure of how well a solute will dissolve in a solvent in specific conditions.

north and south poles of a magnet. Nonpolar molecules do not have poles. Polar molecules form when some atoms in the molecule attract electrons more strongly than other atoms. The electrons gather at one pole, making it negatively charged. The other end of the molecule becomes the positively charged pole.

The general rule is "like dissolves like." A solvent that has polar molecules will dissolve a solute with polar molecules. However, a polar solvent will not dissolve a solute that has nonpolar molecules.

Water is a polar solvent. It dissolves polar solutes, including ionic compounds. Salt dissolves easily in water. However, gasoline is a nonpolar solvent, so salt will not dissolve in it.

Temperature and pressure also affect solubility. Temperature has a stronger effect than pressure. In general, the higher the temperature the more solute that will dissolve in a solvent. Several factors determine exactly how temperature affects solubility.

The speed at which a solid solute dissolves in a solvent is affected by three factors: how quickly the solute and solvent are mixed, the temperature, and the total surface area of the solute. A fine powder will dissolve more quickly than a single large piece.

Physical properties

Sometimes the properties of a solution differ from those of the pure solvent. An obvious example is that the solvent may change color when a solute dissolves in it.

Adding a solute may also change the solvent's melting and boiling points. For example, pure water freezes at 32°F (0°C) and boils at 212°F (100°C). However, when salt is dissolved in water, the solution's

melting point goes down and the boiling point goes up. The exact temperatures depend on how much salt is dissolved. For example, seawater freezes at about 0°F (-17.5°C).

The reason why the melting point changes is because the solute gets in the way of the molecules of solvent. In pure liquid water, the molecules are always moving and colliding with each other. When the water is at 32°F (0°C), the molecules begin to cling together when they collide. Soon they freeze into solid ice. However, as molecules join with the ice, others are breaking free and rejoining the liquid. At the freezing point, the same number of molecules freeze as melt. Below the freezing point, more of them freeze than melt, and the piece of ice grows in size.

When salt ions are mixed in, the water molecules cannot collide with each other as often. Some of the time they hit sodium or chloride ions. At 32°F (0°C), the water does not freeze because the molecules do not come together often enough. Those that do form

Fog covers the slopes of a mountain. Fog is a colloid with tiny droplets of water spread out in the air.

into solid ice are outnumbered by the number of molecules turning into liquid, so ice does not build up.

Suspensions

Not all mixtures in nature are solutions. A suspension is a heterogeneous mixture in which large particles are spread throughout a liquid or a gas. The particles are large enough to settle out eventually. If you have ever shaken up a snow globe, the "snow" floating inside it forms a suspension. It slowly settles back to the bottom.

The particles floating in a suspension are large enough to be filtered out. They can also stop light passing through the suspension. For this reason suspensions are cloudy and difficult to see through. A good example of this is muddy water, which is a suspension of tiny grains of soil floating in water.

Suspensions can form from a mixture of solids, liquid, or gases. An aerosol is a suspension of droplets of liquid or grains of solid in a gas. This sort of mixture is created by spray cans. Solids are often suspended in liquids, as we have seen with muddy water, but two liquids can also form a suspension. The liquids must be immiscible, such as oil and water. One of the liquids

TRY THIS

Give it a spin

You can separate the liquid and solid in a suspension in this simple activity. You will need a large empty tin can, such as a coffee can, and some string. Ask an adult to help—and watch out, you might get wet!

1 Ask an adult to make two small holes in the can. The holes should be opposite each other near to the rim. Make sure the can's rim does not have a dangerous sharp edge.
2 Tie the string through the holes to make a long handle.
3 Fill the can about half full of water and add a handful of soil. Stir the water to mix in the soil and form a suspension.
4 Take the can outside into an area with plenty of space. Swing it around by the string for at least 20 times. Be sure to hold on tightly to the string.
5 Without shaking the can, pour some of the water from the can into a glass and observe. If the water is still very cloudy, spin the can around again several more times.

The fine particles in the soil form a suspension in the water. When the can is swung, the spinning pushes the particles toward the bottom, speeding up the settling process. The can and string are a simple centrifuge. Centrifuges are spinning machines used to remove suspended substances from liquids or gases.

forms into tiny droplets, which are suspended in the other. This sort of suspension is called an emulsion.

Colloids

Colloids are mixtures that share the properties of both solutions and suspensions. The particles in a colloid are spread out through the solvent. They are larger than molecules or ions, but they are not heavy enough to settle. They are also too small to be filtered. Colloids are common in nature. Milk, mayonnaise, and smoke are all colloids.

THE SOLID STATE

A solid is the least energetic form of a substance. Inside a solid, atoms are all linked together, giving it a fixed shape.

Solids are around us everywhere. The ground is solid, buildings are solid, your shoes are solid, and even this book is a solid. According to the kinetic theory—the theory that describes the movement of atoms and molecules—a solid's atoms are constantly moving. However, you have already read about how the atoms in solids are held in place, and this is what gives them their fixed shape. So, instead of moving around like the molecules in a liquid or gas, the molecules in a solid vibrate back and forth around a central position.

Solids have certain properties related to the arrangement of their atoms. Because the particles of a solid are held firmly together, solids have a definite volume and shape. Unlike liquids or gases, in which the atoms or molecules are able to move, the volume and shape of a solid do not change much with temperature or pressure.

Crystalline solids

The most common types of solids are called crystalline solids. They are more simply known as just crystals. Crystalline solids have highly ordered, repeating rows

Most naturally occurring solids are crystals. Inside crystals, the molecules are arranged in a fixed repeating pattern. This gives each crystal its ordered shape.

of particles. These form a structure called a lattice. Table salt, sugar, bath salts, and snow are examples of everyday crystalline solids. Almost all precious gems are crystalline solids, too.

Every crystal has a specific lattice structure. Many of a crystal's properties, such as how hard it is, are defined by how the lattice is put together. Chemists describe the lattice's pattern by selecting the smallest grouping of particles. This grouping is called the unit cell. The lattice is built of many unit cells linked together in a fixed pattern.

Chemists have determined that there are just seven shapes for a unit cell: cubic, hexagonal, rhombohedral, orthorhombic, tetragonal, monoclinic, or triclinic in shape. All crystals are built from one such shell.

SCIENCE WORDS

- **Amorphous:** Something that lacks a definite structure or shape.
- **Crystal:** A solid made of regular repeating patterns of atoms.
- **Solution:** A mixture of substances, where all ingredients are mixed evenly.
- **Supercooled liquid:** An extremely viscous liquid that flows so slowly it can hold its shape like a solid.
- **Viscous:** A viscous liquid is one that is not very runny and flows slowly.

Natural solids

Crystals are very common in nature. Most nonliving solids are composed of crystals. Crystals are perhaps most familiar as the minerals in rocks. In nature, crystals grow from molten (melted) rock or solutions of saturated water. Some types of crystals can grow to a very large size. Single crystals have been found that are as big as a house and weigh many tons.

When crystals grow, they usually follow the same shape as their unit cell. For example, iron pyrite, a shiny gold-colored crystal also known as fool's gold, has a cube-shaped unit cell. Iron pyrite crystals are also cubes. Emerald crystals have a hexagon-shaped unit cell. This is a six-sided shape, and emeralds are often this shape, too.

Three of the unit cells found in crystal lattices. A hexagonal unit cell (1) has 14 particles arranged in a shape with eight faces. Two of the faces are six-sided hexagons. Cubic crystals (2) have six square faces. The cube can contain eight, nine, or 14 particles (shown here). The rhombohedral cell (3) has eight particles that make a six-faced shape. Each face is a rhombus.

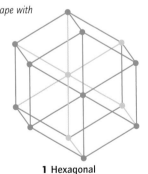

1 Hexagonal

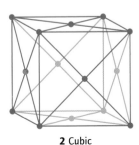

2 Cubic

3 Rhombohedral

TRY THIS

Salt crystals

Crystals are made up of repeating patterns of atoms called unit cells. These cells are joined together in a larger, repeating pattern to form a structure called a lattice. The lattice can be broken down into smaller and smaller pieces, but each piece will still have the same repeating structure of unit cells.

1 Sprinkle some table-salt crystals onto a dark surface. Look through a magnifying glass at them. What shape are they?

2 Sprinkle some pieces of rock salt onto a dark surface. Observe the crystals with a magnifying glass. How does the shape of the crystals compare to the table salt?

3 Break up one of the rock-salt crystals with a hammer. Look at the crystals with the magnifying glass. How do they look now? You should see all types of salt have the same cube-shaped crystals. When you shatter the large cubes of rock salt, you will see that it breaks into smaller cubes.

When crystals break, they tend to break along the links between the unit cells. So, crystals tend to break into certain shapes. Many minerals look very similar. One of the ways a geologist can identify a mineral is by looking at the way its crystal breaks apart.

Amorphous solids

The word amorphous means "without shape." It is used to describe objects that do not have a definite shape, but can take many shapes. Some solids are described as amorphous. They do not have particles arranged in an ordered lattice. Common examples of amorphous solids are plastics and rubber.

Without a lattice structure, amorphous solids have different properties from crystals. For example, most crystals are hard and shatter easily when they are hit. The bits of broken crystal are also the same shape. Amorphous solids tend to be more flexible. If they are broken, the pieces are all different shapes and sizes.

Some amorphous solids, such as glass, are actually supercooled liquids. Rather than being thought of as solids, they can be thought of as extremely viscous liquids. These liquids are so viscous that they do not flow and can hold their shape like a solid. However, like a liquid, the materials can take any shape.

This link to liquids is also shown when amorphous solids are heated. Crystalline solids have a fixed melting point. At this temperature, the whole crystal turns quickly into a liquid. When amorphous solids are heated, they become soft and might flow into a different shape before they finally melt into runny liquid.

Bonding in solids

The physical properties of gases and liquids are explained by the strength of the forces between molecules. These forces also explain the physical properties of solids. Solids have a number of physical properties. These include hardness, ability to conduct electricity, and melting point. Each of these properties depends on the strength of the forces holding the solid together.

Metallic solids

Metals are common solids. Three-quarters of all elements are metals. Metals usually have a small number of valence electrons available for bonding. Valence electrons are those in the outer shell of an atom. These are the electrons involved in chemical bonds. When metal atoms form into a lattice, the valence electrons break free of the atoms and move freely inside the solid. The free electrons act as a "glue"

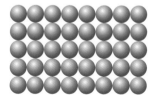

A crystalline solid has molecules arranged in an ordered pattern.

In an amorphous solid, the molecules are all linked together, but are arranged in a random pattern.

that holds the metal atoms together. The electrons can be made to flow in one direction, forming an electric current. Metals are excellent conductors. As well as carrying electricity, metals also conduct heat well.

Metals have two other properties: malleability and ductility. A malleable material can be shaped into thin sheets by beating. Ductile materials can be drawn into wire. Both of these properties result from the way the free electrons glue the metal atoms together.

Alloys

Metals are very useful. They are very strong and can be molded into any shape. We use metals for a wide variety of objects, including cars, tools, wires, and jewelry. Sometimes a pure metal does not have the properties needed for a given task. It may be too soft or not flexible enough. One way to make a metal more useful is to mix it with other metals, and make an alloy. Brass is an alloy of copper and zinc. Some alloys contain nonmetals. Steel is an alloy of iron and several other metals and also contains small amounts of carbon.

Molecular solids

Many solids are made of molecules. Molecules are groups of two or more atoms bonded together. A few elements form molecular solids, including sulfur and iodine. Most molecular solids are compounds. Compounds form when two or more elements react with each other. Their atoms bond together to make a molecule. Sugar is an example of a compound that forms a molecular solid.

Molecular solids are held together by the forces between molecules. In general, molecular solids are soft and melt at low temperatures. This is because the forces between the molecules tend to be weak. Most do not conduct electricity or heat well.

Ionic solids

Some compounds are formed from ions. Ions are atoms that have lost or gained electrons during a chemical reaction. Ions that have lost electrons have a positive charge. Ions that have gained electrons have a negative charge.

Opposite charges attract each other, and like charges repel each other. An ion in a solid is attracted to another ion with the opposite charge. This attraction is what holds ionic solids together. However, the ions are also repelling those with the same charge.

Ionic solids are crystalline. The ions are arranged in a lattice. Inside the lattice, the ions are arranged so ions with opposite charges are as close together as possible. Ions with the same charge are as far apart as possible.

Ionic solids are hard because of their crystalline lattice. Also, because the ionic bonds are so strong, the solids have high melting points, usually much higher than molecular solids. Ionic solids are poor conductors because the ions cannot move.

The simplest ionic solids are made of two ions, one positive and the other negative. For example, table salt (sodium chloride) has one positively charged sodium ion for every negatively charged chloride ion.

Strong solids

Some solids have atoms strongly bonded to each other with covalent bonds. Covalent bonds are formed when atoms share their valence electrons. Many covalent solids are molecular. However, some are crystalline. The covalent bonds connect all the atoms to form a lattice. The lattice is a very strong structure that is difficult to break. This type of solid is called a covalent-network solid. The physical properties of covalent-network solids include a high melting point. Diamonds are an example of covalent-network solids.

PURE GOLD

The purity of gold and other precious metals is measured in karats. Pure gold has 24 karats. Jewelry is seldom made of pure gold, because it is very soft and could be dented or bent easily. Most jewelry is made from a gold alloy, which contains copper and other metals to make it harder. You often see jewelry identified as 18 karat, 14 karat, or 10 karat. The number of karats shows the percentage of gold in the alloy. Twenty-four-karat gold is 100 percent gold. Jewelry made from 18-karat gold contains 75 percent gold, while 12-karat gold is just 50 percent gold. The percentage is arrived at using the following equation:

(Number of karats ÷ 24) x 100 = percentage of
        pure gold

So, for 18-karat gold the equation looks like this

(18 ÷ 24) x 100 = 75 percent

For 12-karat gold the value is

(12 ÷ 24) x 100 = 50 percent

The mask of Tutankhamen, the Egyptian king who was buried 3,300 years ago. The mask is made from pure (24-karat) gold.

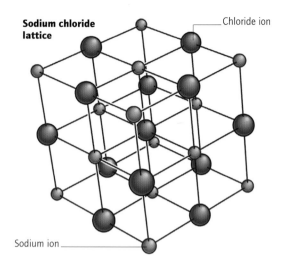

Sodium chloride lattice

Chloride ion

Sodium ion

Solid common salt is made of a lattice of sodium and chloride ions. The lattice has a cubic structure.

Metalloids

The metalloids are a small group of elements that have some of the properties of metals and some of the properties of nonmetals. Metalloids include silicon and arsenic. One property of metalloids is that they conduct electricity, but only in certain conditions. Therefore these materials are called semiconductors. Semiconductors have become important since the 1960s. They are used in electronic devices, such as transistors, which control the flow of electricity around a circuit. Electronics make it possible to build small computers, cell phones, and similar machines.

Semiconductors form covalent-network solids. The atoms are arranged into a lattice. Inside a pure

A cloud of carbon dioxide gas subliming from a piece of dry ice (solid carbon dioxide). Carbon dioxide is actually colorless, but in this case the gas is so cold that it makes the water vapor in the air form a mist of tiny droplets. Since it is a heavy gas, it sinks to the floor.

semiconductor, there are just the right number of electrons to form covalent bonds between all the atoms. However, the electrons are held only loosely in these bonds. A few escape from the bonds and can flow through the solid to conduct electricity. The empty places, known as holes, left by the missing electrons can also move about. The holes behave like movable positive charges.

The way semiconductors conduct electricity can be controlled by adding atoms of other elements. This process is known as doping. Doping fills in the gaps in the lattice of metalloid atoms with an atom of a different element. For example, pure silicon can conduct only a small amount of electricity. If silicon is doped with phosphorus, four of the five electrons of the phosphorus atom bond with silicon atoms. The fifth electron is left free. This free electron is able to move through the solid and carry a current.

SCIENCE WORDS

- **Compound:** A substance formed in a chemical reaction when the atoms of two or more elements bond into a molecule.
- **Ion:** An atom that has lost or gained electrons. Ions have either a positive or negative charge.
- **Molecule:** A group of two or more bonded atoms, forming the smallest unit of a substance.

Expansion

The change from a liquid to a solid is called freezing, and the change from a solid to a liquid is called melting. Before they melt, solids expand as they are heated. As the solid gets hotter, the atoms inside vibrate more, and the distance between the atoms increases. As a result, the entire solid expands. Crystalline and molecular solids tend to expand only a small amount. In general, metals expand the most.

Solid to gas

A few solids do not melt. Instead they change from a solid directly into a gas, in a process called sublimation. Evaporation is when a liquid turns to a gas. In this process, all the atoms or molecules separate from each other and move around independently. Under some circumstances, the molecules in a solid have enough energy to become a gas in the same way. Molecular solids are the most likely to sublime. As they are held together by weak forces between the molecules, this makes it easier for individual molecules to break free and form a gas. Iodine is a shiny gray molecular solid, but when heated it sublimes into a deep-purple gas.

TRY THIS

Formula fun

Use the information in the box below to make the chemical formulas for these ionic compounds:

- calcium oxide
- sodium phosphate
- calcium phosphate

Answers

CaO (One Ca^{2+} and one O_2^{-})

Na_3PO_4 (Three Na^+ and one PO_4^{3-})

$Ca_3(PO_4)_2$ (Three Ca^{2+} and two PO_4^{3-})

Water ice can sometimes sublime. If you leave an ice cube in the freezer for a long time, it can sublime. The air inside the freezer has very little water vapor in it. This makes it easier for molecules of water to break off from the solid ice and form vapor. (If the air was already filled with water vapor, the ice would not sublime as easily.)

TAKING CHARGE OF IONS

When writing the formula for an ionic compound, you need to know the charge of the ions involved. Metal ions always have a positive charge and nonmetals always produce negatively charged ions.

The name of the ion can provide a clue about the charge. Positive ions have the same name as the atoms (for example, sodium ion), but negative ions often have a different name (for example, chloride ion).

When writing the formula, the charge of the compound must be equal to zero. For example, potassium chloride is made up of potassium ions and chloride ions. A potassium ion has a charge of +1 and a chloride ion has a charge of –1. Therefore, one of each ion combines to form the molecule, which has the formula KCl.

Aluminum chloride is made up of aluminum and chloride ions. Because the aluminum ion has a charge of +3 and the chloride ion has a charge of –1, an aluminum ion combines with three chloride ions. The chemical formula for aluminum chloride is $AlCl_3$. The number 3 shows that the molecule has three chloride ions for one aluminum ion. Together the chloride ions have a total charge of –3, which balances the +3 charge of the aluminum ion.

Ion	Symbol	Charge
sodium	Na^+	+1
potassium	K^+	+1
calcium	Ca^{2+}	+2
aluminum	Al^{3+}	+3
chloride	Cl^-	–1
oxide	O^{2-}	–2
phosphate	PO_4^{3-}	–3

Most substances have a state in which they normally exist, either as solids, liquids, or gases. They can be made to change state by the addition or removal of energy, usually kinetic energy in the form of heat.

A change in state, or phase change, happens when a substance turns from one phase to another, for example, when a solid becomes a liquid. A phase change happens when particles in solids, liquids, or gases either combine or break up. These phase changes always involve a change in energy.

Energy and phase changes

When a substance undergoes a phase change from solid to liquid or liquid to gas, the particles must overcome the intermolecular forces—the forces between molecules—in the original state. The energy particles use to overcome the intermolecular forces is kinetic energy. The source of this kinetic energy is heat. As heat is added to a substance, the particles absorb the energy and increase their own kinetic energy. Remember that temperature is a measure of the average kinetic energy. Therefore, there is a temperature increase when more energy is added.

This spiderweb is hung with beads of dew. Dew forms when moist air cools or hits a cold surface and condenses (turns into a liquid). This switch from air to water represents a change of state, or phase change.

When a substance undergoes a phase change from gas to liquid or liquid to solid, energy is also important. But the particles must lose kinetic energy. The particles move more slowly as the phase changes. Because energy is given up, this is called an endothermic process.

Changing a substance from a liquid to a gas requires more energy than changing the same substance from a solid to a liquid. Gases have the highest energy of the three states of matter. The substance must gain enough kinetic energy for the particle to completely overcome the intermolecular forces. Substances with stronger intermolecular forces

SCIENCE WORDS

- **Endothermic:** A chemical reaction in which heat is absorbed and the surrounding temperature falls.
- **Exothermic:** A chemical reaction in which heat is released and the surrounding temperature goes up.
- **Heat of fusion:** The amount of energy needed to turn a solid into a liquid.
- **Heat of vaporization:** The amount of energy needed to turn a liquid into a gas.

have much higher boiling points because more energy is required for the particles to become a gas.

The amount of energy needed to change a solid to a liquid is called the heat of fusion. The amount of energy required to change a liquid to a gas is called the heat of vaporization.

Heat of fusion

The heat of fusion is the amount of energy needed to break the intermolecular bonds in a solid to turn it into a liquid. The change in phase from a solid to a liquid does not involve a change in temperature. While a substance is melting, the temperature stays constant, with the result that the particles do not actually change their kinetic energy. There is not a change in the kinetic energy until the phase change is complete.

Freezing

The heat of fusion is also the amount of heat given off when a substance changes from a liquid to a solid. For most substances, the particles in the solid state are much closer together than in the liquid state. This means there are more molecules packed into a given volume in a solid than a liquid. The solid form of a substance therefore has a higher density than the liquid form. That explains why the solid phase for most substances will sink in its liquid phase.

Water is one of the exceptions to this rule. When water freezes, the water molecules actually move farther apart than they are in the liquid phase. This occurs because of the strong intermolecular forces in water caused by hydrogen bonding. This explains why ice floats in water. Ice is actually about 9 percent less dense than water. Because water expands as it freezes, it is important to leave space in a container of water before freezing. If a full container is sealed, the water will expand and cause the container to burst.

When a solid is heated and it reaches the melting point, the temperature remains constant as the phase changes. Scientists can easily measure this temperature for substances that do not have very high or very low

TRY THIS

Expanding ice
1 Press a piece of clay onto the bottom of a bowl.
2 Push a drinking straw into the clay so that the straw stands up.
3 Add several drops of food coloring to some water. Use an eyedropper to fill the drinking straw until it is about half full of colored water.
4 Mark the level of the water in the straw with the permanent marker.
5 Place the bowl in the freezer for at least 4 hours.
6 Remove the bowl from the freezer and observe how the level in the straw has changed as the water froze. As the water froze, the ice expanded. This should have caused the level of the water in the straw to increase.

Mark the level of the water with a permanent marker.

The water in the straw has risen because water expands when it becomes ice. Almost every other substance contracts when it freezes.

melting points. The melting point is the same temperature as the freezing point. When a liquid is cooled and it reaches the freezing point, the temperature remains constant until the phase changes. The melting point or freezing point of a substance may also be useful in determining the exact nature of a substance. Each substance has its own melting point.

Heat of vaporization

As with melting, the temperature of this phase change remains constant until the phase change is complete. When a liquid reaches its boiling point, the particles do not gain kinetic energy. Instead, the particles in the liquid use the energy to overcome the intermolecular forces. Once all the liquid has changed to a gas, the temperature rises again.

Boiling

A liquid boils when its vapor pressure is equal to the atmospheric pressure. For example, at sea level, water boils at 212°F (100°C). As elevation above sea level

SCIENCE WORDS

- **Condensation:** The change of state from a gas to a liquid.
- **Evaporation:** The change of state from a liquid to a gas when the liquid is at a temperature below its boiling point.
- **Intermolecular force:** The weak attraction between the molecules of a substance.
- **Pressure:** The force pushing on an area.
- **Vapor:** The gas form of a substance that exists below the substance's critical temperature and can still be liquefied.

increases, the atmospheric pressure decreases. This decrease in atmospheric pressure means that the temperature water boils at also decreases. This decrease can become significant when cooking at higher elevations. Many recipes include directions for cooking the food at higher elevations.

BOILING AND EVAPORATION

When a liquid is boiled (a), the molecules gain kinetic energy and can escape from the surface and form vapor bubbles in the liquid. In evaporation (b), molecules leave the liquid without heat being added. The liquid loses energy and gets cooler (c).

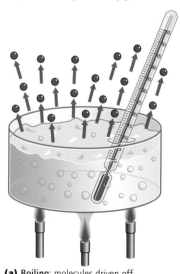
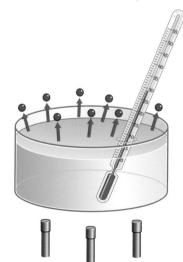
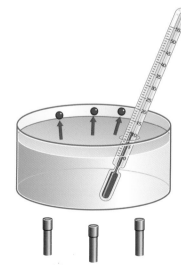

(a) Boiling: molecules driven off

(b) Evaporation: molecules escape

(c) Evaporation: causes cooling

If the atmospheric pressure is increased, the boiling point of water also increases. Some cooks use a device called a pressure cooker to increase the pressure and thereby increase the temperature at which water boils. Because the temperature is increased, the food cooks much faster.

Cooling by evaporation

The changing of a liquid to a gas requires energy. That is an endothermic process. This process is very important to people. When you work hard or exercise, your body generates heat. Your body must rid itself of this excess heat. One way your body does this is by sweating. When your body heats up, sweat covers your skin. Heat from your body warms the sweat causing it to begin evaporating. Because evaporation is an endothermic process, the sweat molecules absorb heat, and this creates a cooling effect on the body.

Cooling by evaporation (evaporative cooling) is a good way for your body to get rid of excess heat. However, cooling by evaporation does not always work. One factor that affects evaporative cooling is humidity. Humidity is the amount of water vapor present in the air. When the humidity is high, the amount of water vapor present in the air can approach the saturation point (maximum possible). In these conditions, air cannot hold any more water, and sweat cannot evaporate. The most ideal condition for evaporative cooling is when the air has very little water vapor in it.

Changing phases

Like all matter, water exists in three different states—solid, liquid, and gas. Water is familiar to us in all its different states. Water as a solid is called ice, as a liquid it is just called water, and as a gas it is called water vapor or steam. As water changes between states, each of these changes has a name. When water changes from a solid to a liquid, it melts. When water changes from a liquid to a solid, it freezes. When water changes from a liquid to a gas, it boils. When water changes from a gas to a liquid, it condenses.

Suppose you took an ice cube from the freezer. If the freezer is at 23°F (-5°C), the ice cube will be at the same temperature. If the ice cube is placed in a pan and heated on the stove, energy is added. The ice cube absorbs energy and its temperature increases steadily. When the ice cube reaches its melting point, the temperature does not change. Energy is being used to change the solid to a liquid so the temperature remains constant until all the ice melts.

Once the ice melts, the temperature rises again. The temperature of the water continues to rise until it reaches the boiling point. Once the water starts boiling, the temperature remains constant until all the water has changed to water vapor or steam. After all the water has boiled and turned to steam, the temperature of the steam increases as more energy is added.

When energy is removed from steam, the reverse happens. The temperature of the steam decreases until it begins to condense (change from gas to liquid). The temperature is constant until all the steam condenses into liquid water. The temperature continues to decrease until the water reaches its freezing point. As the water changes from a liquid to a solid, the temperature remains constant. Once all the water has turned to ice, the temperature continues to fall.

TRY THIS

Chill out
Evaporative cooling is an efficient way to lower temperature.

1 Pour a little rubbing alcohol onto a cotton ball.
2 Squeeze out the excess alcohol and lightly wrap the cotton ball around the bulb of a thermometer.
3 Blow on the cotton ball and watch what happens to the temperature on the thermometer. The alcohol absorbs energy so it can evaporate. This causes the temperature to decrease.

GLOSSARY

Alchemist Person who tried to change one substance into another using a combination of primitive chemistry and magic.

Alpha particle The nucleus of a helium atom. This particle has two protons and two neutrons.

Atom The smallest independent building block of matter.

Atomic mass number The number of protons and neutrons in an atom's nucleus.

Atomic number The number of protons in a nucleus.

Chemical formula The letters and numbers that represent a chemical compound, such as H_2O for water.

Chemical symbol The letters that represent a chemical, such as "Cl" for chlorine or "Na" for sodium.

Compound A substance formed in a chemical reaction when the atoms of two of more elements bond into a molecule.

Compress To reduce in size or volume by squeezing or exerting pressure.

Condensation The change of state from a gas to a liquid.

Crystal A solid made of regular repeating patterns of atoms.

Dipole attraction The attractive force between charged ends of molecules.

Electrolyte An ionic substance that can conduct electricity.

Electromagnetic radiation The energy emitted by a source, for example, x-rays, ultraviolet light, visible light, heat, or radio waves.

Electromagnetic spectrum The range of energy waves that includes light, heat, and radio waves.

Electron A negatively charged particle that orbits an atom's nucleus.

Element A material that cannot be broken up into simpler ingredients.

Endothermic A chemical reaction in which heat is absorbed and the surrounding temperature falls.

Energy level The electron shells in an atom each represent a different energy level. Those closest to the nucleus have the lowest energy.

Evaporation The change of state from a liquid to a gas when the liquid is at a temperature below its boiling point.

Exothermic A chemical reaction in which heat is released and the surrounding temperature goes up.

Four elements The ancient theory that all matter consisted of only four elements (earth, air, fire, and water) and their combinations.

Gas State in which particles are not joined and are free to move in any direction.

Heat of fusion The amount of energy needed to turn a solid into a liquid.

Heat of vaporization The amount of energy needed to turn a liquid into a gas.

Heterogeneous mixture A mixture in which ingredients are not spread evenly.

Homogeneous mixture A mixture in which substances are spread out evenly.

Hydrogen bond Dipole attraction that always involves a hydrogen atom.

Immiscible When substances cannot mix.

Insoluble When a substance will not dissolve in another substance.

Intermolecular bond Weak bond between one molecule and another.

Intermolecular force The weak attraction between the molecules of a substance.

Intramolecular bond Strong bond between atoms in a molecule.

Ion An atom that has lost or gained an electron or electrons.

Ionization The formation of ions by adding or removing electrons from atoms.

Isotopes Atoms with the same atomic number, but a different atomic mass.

Kinetic energy The energy of a moving particle.

Kinetic theory Theory that describes the properties of matter in terms of the motion of particles.

Liquid State in which particles are loosely bonded and are able to move freely around each other.

Miscible When substances can mix.

Mole The amount of any substance that contains the same number of atoms or molecules as 12 grams of carbon. This number is called the Avogadro number and equals $6.022 * 10^{23}$

Molecule A collection of two or more atoms that are connected by bonds.

Neutron A subatomic particle with no charge located in an atom's nucleus.

Nucleus The central part of an atom, made of protons and neutrons.

Photon A particle that carries a quantity of energy, usually in the form of light.

Pressure The force produced by pressing on something.

Proton A positively charged particle found in an atom's nucleus.

Radiation The products of radioactivity—alpha and beta particles and gamma rays.

Relative atomic mass (RAM) A measure of the mass of an atom compared with the mass of another atom. The values used are the same as those for atomic mass.

Relative molecular mass (RMM) The sum of all the atomic masses of the atoms in a molecule.

Saturated A solution that has the maximum amount of solute dissolved in the solvent.

Shell The orbit of an electron. Each shell can contain a specific number of electrons and no more.

Solid Matter in which particles are held in a rigid arrangement.

Solubility A measure of how well a solute will dissolve in a solvent in specific conditions.

Soluble When a substance can dissolve in another substance.

Solution A mixture of substances, where all ingredients are mixed evenly.

State The form that matter takes—either a solid, a liquid, or a gas.

Subatomic particles Particles that are smaller than an atom.

Supercooled liquid An extremely viscous liquid that flows so slowly it can hold its shape like a solid.

Temperature A measure of the hotness or coldness of a substance.

Van der Waals forces Short-lived forces between atoms and molecules.

Vapor The gas form of a substance that exists below the substance's critical temperature and can still be liquefied.

Viscous A viscous liquid is one that is not very runny and flows slowly.

Volume The space that a solid, liquid, or gas occupies. The SI unit is the cubic meter (m^3).

FURTHER RESEARCH

Books

Atkins, P. W. *The Periodic Kingdom: A Journey into the Land of Chemical Elements*. New York, NY: Barnes & Noble Books, 2007.

Bendick, J., and Wiker, B. *The Mystery of the Periodic Table (Living History Library)*. Bathgate, ND: Bethlehem Books, 2003.

Berg, J. *Biochemistry*. New York, NY: W. H. Freeman, 2006.

Brown, T. E. *et al. Chemistry: The Central Science*. Englewood Cliffs, NJ: Prentice Hall, 2008.

Cobb, C., and Fetterolf, M. L. *The Joy of Chemistry: The Amazing Science of Familiar Things*. Amherst, NY: Prometheus Books, 2010.

Davis, M. *et al. Modern Chemistry*. New York, NY: Holt, 2008.

Gray, Theodore. *Theo Gray's Mad Science: Experiments You Can Do at Home—But Probably Shouldn't*. New York, NY: Black Dog & Leventhal Publishers, 2009.

Greenberg A. *From Alchemy to Chemistry in Picture and Story*. Hoboken, NJ: Wiley, 2007.

Herr, N., and Cunningham, J. *Hands-on Chemistry Activities with Real-Life Applications*. Hoboken, NJ: Jossey-Bass, 2002.

Karukstis, K. K., and Van Hecke, G. R. *Chemistry Connections: The Chemical Basis of Everyday Phenomena*. Burlington, MA: Academic Press, 2003.

Lehninger, A., Cox, M., and Nelson, D. *Lehninger's Principles of Biochemistry*. New York, NY: W. H. Freeman, 2008.

LeMay, E. *et al. Chemistry: Connections to Our Changing World*. New York, NY: Prentice Hall (Pearson Education), 2002.

Levere, T. H. *Transforming Matter: A History of Chemistry from Alchemy to the Buckyball*. Baltimore, MD: The Johns Hopkins University Press, 2001.

Oxlade, C. *Elements and Compounds (Chemicals in Action)*. Chicago, IL: Heinemann, 2008.

Poynter, M. *Marie Curie: Discoverer of Radium (Great Minds of Science)*. Berkeley Heights, NJ: Enslow Publishers, 2007.

Saunders, N. *Fluorine and the Halogens*. Chicago, IL: Heinemann Library, 2005.

Shevick, E., and Wheeler, R. *Great Scientists in Action: Early Life, Discoveries, and Experiments*. Carthage, IL: Teaching & Learning Company, 2004.

Stwertka, A. *A Guide to the Elements*. New York, NY: Oxford University Press, 2002.

Thompson, B. T. *Illustrated Guide to Home Chemistry Experiments: All Lab, No Lecture*. Sebastopol, CA: O'Reilly Media, 2008.

Tiner, J. H. *Exploring the World of Chemistry: From Ancient Metals to High-Speed Computers*. Green Forest, AZ: Master Books, 2000.

Trombley, L., and Williams, F. *Mastering the Periodic Table: 50 Activities on the Elements*. Portland, ME: Walch, 2002.

Walker, P., and Wood, E. *Crime Scene Investigations: Real-life Science Labs for Grades 6–12*. Hoboken, NJ: Jossey-Bass, 2002.

Wilbraham, A., *et al. Chemistry*. New York, NY: Prentice Hall (Pearson Education), 2001.

Woodford, C., and Clowes, M. *Routes of Science: Atoms and Molecules*. San Diego, CA: Blackbirch Press, 2004.

Web sites

The Art and Science of Bubbles
www.sdahq.org/sdakids/bubbles
Information and activities about bubbles.

Chemical Achievers
www.chemheritage.org/classroom/chemach/index.html
Biographical details about leading chemists and their discoveries.

The Chemistry of Fireworks
library.thinkquest.org/15384/chem/chem.htm
Information on the chemical reactions that occur when a firework explodes.

Chemistry: The Periodic Table Online
www.webelements.com
Detailed information about elements.

Chemistry Tutor
library.thinkquest.org/2923
A series of Web pages that help with chemistry assignments.

Chem4Kids
www.chem4Kids.com
Includes sections on matter, atoms, elements, and biochemistry.

Chemtutor Elements
www.chemtutor.com/elem.htm
Information on a selection of the elements.

Eric Weisstein's World of Chemistry
scienceworld.wolfram.com/chemistry
Chemistry information divided into eight broad topics, from chemical reactions to quantum chemistry.

General Chemistry Help
chemed.chem.purdue.edu/genchem
General information on chemistry plus movie clips of key concepts.

IUPAC
www.iupac.org/
Web site of the International Union of Pure and Applied Chemistry.

Molecular Models
chemlabs.uoregon.edu/GeneralResources/models/models.html
A site that explains the use of molecular models.

New Scientist
www.newscientist.com/home.ns
Online science magazine providing general news on scientific developments.

The Physical Properties of Minerals
mineral.galleries.com/minerals/physical.htm
Methods for identifying minerals.

Scientific American
www.sciam.com
Latest news on developments in science and technology.

Virtual Laboratory: Ideal Gas Laws
zebu.uoregon.edu/nsf/piston.html
University of Oregon site showing simulation of ideal gas laws.

INDEX

Words and page numbers in **bold type** indicate main references to the various topics. Page numbers in *italic* refer to illustrations; those underlined refer to definitions. Page numbers in brackets indicate box features.